AF254765

The AI-Equipped Teacher

Practical Tools and Strategies to Beat Burnout and Build a Sustainable K-12 Career

By: Patty R Adams

2026

rendering of legal, financial, medical, or professional advice. The content within this book has been derived from various sources. Please consult a licensed professional before attempting any techniques outlined in this book.

By reading this document, the reader agrees that under no circumstances is the author responsible for any losses, direct or indirect, that are incurred as a result of the use of the information contained within this document, including, but not limited to, errors, omissions, or inaccuracies.

Table of Contents

Thank You for Reading!

I hope you find **The AI-Equipped Teacher** helpful and enjoyable!

Your feedback is invaluable to me and helps others discover this book.

If you could take a moment to leave a review, I'd greatly appreciate it. Scan the QR code below to leave your review:

Thank you!

Patty

Visit the Cantelune Press website for more compassionate books that meet you where you are! https://cantelunepress.com/

Introduction

You are not failing. You need to hear that right now, before you read another word.

You are not lazy. You are not inadequate. You are not doing something wrong. You are simply under-equipped for a job that has asked far too much of teachers for far too long.

If you are reading this book, chances are you chose teaching because you genuinely love kids and believed you could make a difference. And you still do, somewhere beneath the exhaustion.

But lately, that belief has been buried under an avalanche of lesson plans, grading, parent emails, data entry, and administrative tasks that never seem to end. You leave school drained every single day. You bring work home every single night. You spend your weekends trying desperately to catch up, and by Sunday evening, the weight of Monday morning already sits heavy on your chest.

Your personal life is suffering. Maybe you've canceled plans with friends more times than you can count. Maybe you've snapped at someone you love because you were too tired to be patient. Maybe you've sat in your car in the school parking lot and cried because you cannot remember the last time you felt like yourself.

And the worst part is the guilt. You feel guilty when you're not working because there is always more to do. You feel resentful when you're working because you've given up everything else. You're starting to wonder if you made the right career choice – not because you stopped loving teaching, but because the job has swallowed your whole life.

You are not alone in this. Thousands of teachers across the country are living this exact same reality right now. They're staying up until midnight writing lesson plans. They're grading papers during lunch. They are answering parent emails at the dinner table. They are sacrificing their health, their relationships, and their joy because they were told that this is what it means to be a good teacher.

That belief is a lie, and it is destroying the profession from the inside out.

But you don't have to choose between being a great teacher and having a great life. You just need the right tools. This book exists to hand you those tools. Real, practical, immediately usable strategies that will give you back your evenings, your weekends, and your sense of control.

And here is what might surprise you most: the key to getting your life back is not working harder or becoming more efficient at doing everything yourself. The key is AI.

If you just felt your stomach tighten at that word, you are exactly who this book is for. AI sounds complicated and intimidating. And worst of all, it sounds like one more thing you do not have time to learn.

Maybe you've heard colleagues mention it in passing, or your district sent around some vague email about it, but you have no idea where to start. Maybe you're worried it is unethical to use in education, or that it will replace the human connection that makes teaching meaningful in the first place. Maybe you assume it's only for tech-savvy teachers who already have their lives together, and you're barely keeping your head above water as it is.

Simply put, AI is the tool that handles the tasks that drain you so you can pour your energy into the moments that only you can provide.

It writes the first draft of your lesson plans so you can spend your time refining them instead of staring at a blank screen. It generates quiz questions and rubrics so you can focus on giving meaningful feedback instead of drowning in paperwork. It drafts parent emails and permission slips so you can use your words for the conversations that actually matter.

It doesn't take away the heart of teaching. It protects it.

And the best part is that you don't need to be a tech expert to use it. This book will walk you through every single step in plain, everyday language. You are going to learn which tools are worth your time, how to access them, and exactly how to use them to save hours every single week.

But this book is about more than just AI. It's about building a teaching career that doesn't break you. And you are going to walk away with a plan – not just ideas, but a real, actionable plan – for building a 20-plus-year career in education that is both fulfilling and sustainable.

You are going to walk away from this book feeling something you may not have felt in a very long time: hope. Not the fragile, fleeting kind of hope that disappears the moment you walk back into your classroom. Real, grounded, practical hope that comes from knowing you have a plan and the tools to execute it.

You are about to discover that AI is not something to fear. It is the key that unlocks the personal life you thought you had to sacrifice to be a good teacher. You are about to learn that being equipped is far more powerful than being inspired, because equipped means you close this book, open your laptop, and know exactly what to do next. You are about to realize that you can build a teaching career that doesn't consume you, one that allows you to love your job and your life at the same time.

You are enough. You are capable. Your wellbeing matters. Your time matters. Your life outside the classroom matters. And it's time someone handed you the tools to protect all of it while still being the incredible teacher you set out to be.

Let's get started.

Chapter 1. You Didn't Sign Up for This

You chose teaching because you care deeply about students. You believed you could make a difference. And you still do, somewhere beneath the exhaustion.

But lately, that belief is buried under a mountain of demands that never seem to end. You leave school drained every single day. You bring work home every night. Your weekends disappear into planning and grading. Your personal life is suffering.

This is not what you signed up for. You did not become a teacher to spend your evenings formatting worksheets or your Sundays writing lesson plans. You became a teacher to connect with students, to inspire curiosity, to watch young people grow. But the job has swallowed those moments whole, and you're left wondering if you made the right choice.

The Reality of Teacher Burnout: Naming What You're Feeling

What you are experiencing has a name: burnout. And it isn't just in your head. It is a documented crisis affecting educators nationwide.

In 2025, 53% of U.S. teachers reported experiencing burnout at work. That number was even higher the year before – 60% in 2024 – showing some stabilization, but still a staggering reality.

To put that in perspective, only 33% of comparable working adults report burnout. Teachers are burning out at nearly twice the rate of other professionals.

The stress statistics are equally alarming. 62% of teachers reported frequent job-related stress in 2025, compared to just 33% of similar professionals. Even more concerning, 21% of teachers said they struggle to cope with job-related stress.

These aren't just numbers on a page. These are real people – colleagues, friends, maybe you – who are drowning.

Burnout shows up in three distinct ways:

- Emotional exhaustion
- Reduced sense of accomplishment
- Depersonalization

You might recognize these in yourself. The emotional exhaustion is that bone-deep tiredness that doesn't go away after a weekend. The reduced accomplishment is the nagging feeling that nothing you do is ever enough. The depersonalization is the distance you feel creeping in between you and your students, the moments when you catch yourself going through the motions instead of truly connecting.

The causes of this burnout are systemic and relentless. Workload and staffing shortages top the list. 86% of school districts report open positions, and 57% of high-poverty schools are understaffed. This means teachers are covering extra classes, taking on additional duties, and stretching themselves impossibly thin just to keep schools running.

Nationally, over 411,000 teaching positions were either vacant or filled by under-certified educators in mid-2025.

The crisis affects some teachers more than others. Black teachers report 56% frequent stress and 59% burnout, while Hispanic and Latino teachers report 66% stress and 58% burnout – rates significantly higher than their white counterparts. These educators also face higher rates of depression symptoms and intent to leave the profession.

If you see yourself in these statistics, you are responding exactly as any human being would to an unsustainable situation. The system has asked too much of you for too long, and your exhaustion is proof that you've been giving everything you have.

The Two Solutions That Will Change Everything

The good news is that there are two practical, powerful solutions that can transform your daily reality as a teacher. And these are not vague inspirational ideas. These are concrete strategies that will give you back measurable hours every single week and help you build a sustainable career.

- The first solution is harnessing AI to automate administrative workloads.
- The second solution is redirecting the time you reclaim toward high-impact teaching and your own well-being.

Let's start with AI. Right now, 84% of teachers report insufficient time for lesson planning, grading, and paperwork due to overwhelming workloads. These repetitive tasks consume your personal time and erode any hope of work-life balance.

AI tools can systematically reduce these administrative burdens, reclaiming five to eight hours weekly. Districts that have implemented AI report an average time savings of 5.9 hours per week through automation of lesson planning, grading, and communication.

Teachers using platforms like Toddle save eight hours weekly, while others reduce administrative time by five to six hours using tools such as MagicSchool AI, Diffit, and Gradescope.

This is not a small improvement. This is potentially 30 to 50% less time spent on administrative tasks.

AI can generate customized lesson plans, modify materials for diverse learners such as English language learners or students with IEPs, create rubrics, and differentiate instruction. Tools like GradeWithAI and Kuraplan slash planning and grading time by automating standards alignment and formatting. This reduction frees mental bandwidth for the work that actually matters: instruction, relationships, and self-care.

Heather Gauck, a special education teacher in Grand Rapids Public Schools with three decades of experience, used MagicSchool AI to help a struggling fourth grader who could not spell simple words. After the student verbally shared a story idea, Gauck inputted it into the tool, which generated a full narrative. This led to a literacy breakthrough, reduced the student's acting out, and enabled personalized progress. This is what becomes possible when you have the right tools.

Cindy Blackburn, Director of Learning and Engagement at Toddle, confirms that "teachers who use the AI-based educational platform Toddle... are already saving eight hours a week." Another teacher using AI tools shared, "I can now spend that time building relationships with my students and focusing on that deeper instruction."

The second solution is what you do with that reclaimed time. You redirect it toward meaningful classroom impact, professional growth, and personal sustainability. By offloading routine tasks, you can focus on relationship-building, deeper instruction, and creative adaptations – activities AI cannot replicate.

This might look like using AI-generated scaffolds for role-playing real-world scenarios or tailoring lessons for specific student populations. It might mean joining a professional learning community or peer mentoring group, which can reduce burnout by up to 50% through collaboration and reduced isolation. It might mean using ChatGPT for initial lesson ideas and then refining those outputs into personalized plans that reflect your unique teaching style.

Together, these two solutions – AI-driven workload reduction and intentional time redirection – address the root causes of burnout without requiring salary increases or additional staff. They protect teaching's core mission while giving you back your life. Districts adopting AI see improved retention and student outcomes, as teachers shift from exhaustion to empowerment.

This is the path forward. It's practical. It's proven. And it starts today.

What This Book Will Do for You (And What It Won't)

Before you go any further, you need to know exactly what this book will and will not do for you.

This book will not solve every problem. It will not address systemic issues such as inadequate compensation, excessive class sizes, or insufficient institutional support. Technology's promise to solve educational challenges has historically "failed to deliver in recent years." AI is a powerful tool, but it is not a magic wand that fixes broken systems.

This book will not replace human connection. Your true advantage as an educator "lies not in competing with AI's efficiency, but in fostering values like empathy, ethical reasoning, and complex problem-solving – skills machines cannot replicate." AI tools remain "a resource" within "authentic assessments and opportunities" centered around human creativity and emotional intelligence.

This book will not offer simple, one-size-fits-all solutions. Integrating AI involves "productive tensions" and "uncharted territory." You will need to adapt the frameworks in this book to your specific context, your students, and your teaching style. There are no universally applicable shortcuts.

This book will not eliminate the need for ongoing learning. "AI is only going to get better and more ubiquitous: specialized AI tools are about to proliferate," requiring ongoing adaptation. What you learn here is a foundation, not a finish line.

What this book will do is validate the genuine crisis you are facing while offering a clear, practical, compassionate path forward.

You "have a responsibility to prepare students for the future they will inhabit," but that responsibility must be balanced with your own wellbeing. Your students gain access to a less burned-out teacher and develop AI literacy and the ability to use AI as a partner – essential skills for all students.

As one educator put it, "AI does not have to be the enemy of learning. If guided properly, it can become one of the greatest allies education has ever seen." This book will guide you in making AI your ally, not your replacement. It will help you reclaim your time, restore your energy, and remember why you became a teacher in the first place.

You did not sign up to sacrifice your entire life for this job. You signed up to teach, to inspire, to make a difference. The tools and strategies in this book will help you do exactly that – without losing yourself in the process. The path forward is clear. The tools are within reach. And you are not walking this road alone.

Turn the page, and let's begin.

Chapter 2. Remember Why You Started

Close your eyes for a moment and think back to the day you decided to become a teacher. What was it that made you say yes to this profession?

Maybe it was a teacher who believed in you when no one else did. Maybe it was the moment you watched a child's face light up when something finally clicked. Maybe it was the quiet conviction that you could make a difference in a world that desperately needed people who cared.

Whatever it was, that moment mattered. It was real. It was powerful. And it brought you here.

But somewhere between that moment and today, something changed. The work that once filled you with purpose now leaves you depleted. The students you adore feel like one more demand you cannot meet. The evenings you once spent with family or friends are now consumed by lesson plans and grading. You are exhausted in a way that sleep doesn't fix. You feel guilty when you're not working and resentful when you are.

And the question that keeps you awake at night is, *Did I make the right choice?*

You did. You absolutely did. But passion alone is not enough to sustain a career in education. You also need the right tools, the right boundaries, and the right understanding of what is happening to you right now.

It's about finding the thread that leads back to the person you were when you said yes – and building a teaching life that honors both that person and the one you are becoming.

Your Original Why: Reconnecting With Your Teaching Purpose

Teaching purpose originates from intrinsic motivation to impact students' lives and foster growth, serving as the foundational "why" that draws educators to the profession. It's the entire reason you're here.

Reconnecting with your original passion involves reflecting on initial motivations – the joy of witnessing student breakthroughs or the desire to inspire. And don't worry, your original why is still there. It has not disappeared. It has just been buried under layers of exhaustion and obligation. The first step in reconnecting is giving yourself permission to remember what teaching felt like before it felt like drowning.

Start by asking yourself these questions:

- What was the specific moment I knew I wanted to teach?
- What did I believe I could offer students that no one else could?
- What kind of teacher did I imagine I would be?

Let yourself remember the version of you who walked into this profession with hope instead of dread. And this is not about nostalgia. It's anchoring yourself to something real. When you're drowning in grading at ten o'clock on a Sunday night, your original why becomes the lifeline that reminds you this work is worth protecting – not by doing more of it, but by doing it differently.

Your why is not just a memory. It's a compass. And right now, you need it more than ever.

Exhaustion vs. Burnout: Knowing the Difference

Temporary exhaustion arises from acute stressors – intense grading periods, disruptions, or high-demand weeks – and dissipates with short-term recovery like rest or boundary-setting. This is the kind of tired that comes after parent-teacher conferences, state testing week, the school play or the field trip or the end of the quarter.

It is real. It is legitimate. And it goes away when you sleep, when you take a weekend off, when you finally get a break.

True burnout emerges gradually from sustained demands, manifesting in cynicism, reduced efficacy, and detachment from core purpose. Burnout is not just being tired. It's waking up tired. It's feeling exhausted even after a full night of sleep. It's looking at your lesson plans and feeling nothing – no excitement, no creativity, just the heavy weight of one more thing you have to get through.

Burnout is when you stop caring about the things that used to matter most, when you find yourself snapping at students you genuinely love, when you dread Monday morning before the weekend even starts.

Here is how to tell the difference:

- **Temporary exhaustion** resolves with rest. You take a sick day, you sleep in on Saturday, you spend Sunday doing something you love, and by Monday you feel human again.

- **Burnout** does not respond to rest. You take a week off and come back feeling just as empty as when you left.

- **Temporary exhaustion** makes you tired.

- **Burnout** makes you cynical. You start to resent your students, your colleagues, your administrators. You stop believing that anything you do makes a difference.

- **Temporary exhaustion** affects your energy.

- **Burnout** affects your identity. You start to question whether you're cut out for this work, and whether you ever were.

- **Temporary exhaustion** might give you a headache or make your shoulders tense.

- **Burnout** shows up as chronic fatigue unresponsive to sleep, insomnia or oversleeping, frequent illnesses, gastrointestinal issues, and persistent back pain. Your body is not just tired. It is breaking down.

Burnout doesn't announce itself. It creeps in quietly until one day you realize you cannot remember the last time you felt genuinely happy in your classroom. But the good news is that once you can name it, you can address it.

The Moment Things Shifted: Identifying When Joy Became Overwhelm

Teachers are conditioned to believe that struggling means failing, that asking for help is a sign of weakness, that good teachers just figure it out. This culture of silence makes it nearly impossible to recognize when normal stress has crossed the line into something more dangerous.

The "moment things shifted" often correlates with administrative burdens, student behavior challenges, or eroded work-life balance.

For some teachers, it was a specific event: the meeting where you were told your best was not good enough, the parent email that accused you of not caring, the day you realized you had not taken a lunch break in three weeks.

For others, it was more gradual: the slow accumulation of one more initiative, one more expectation, one more thing added to your plate without anything being taken off.

The moment things shifted is not always dramatic. Sometimes it's quiet. Sometimes it is the morning you wake up and realize you do not want to go to work – not because you have a hard day ahead, but because you cannot remember the last time you wanted to be there at all.

If you are reading this and recognizing yourself, please know that the shift is not permanent. You have not lost your passion forever. You've just buried it under too much weight. So let's help you become the teacher you already are – just with better tools, better boundaries, and better support.

Finding the Thread That Leads Back to Passion

Reconnecting involves tracing back to core motivations to rebuild emotional resilience. The thread that leads back to passion is not a straight line. It's messy. It requires honesty about what has been lost and courage to imagine what could be different. But it is there. And it's worth finding.

Start by revisiting your "why." Identify inspiring moments that initially drew you to teaching to reignite motivation. Go back through your memory and find the moments that made you believe this work mattered. Maybe it was a student who wrote you a note saying you were the only teacher who ever listened. Maybe it was the day you realized you could explain a concept in a way that finally made sense. Maybe it was watching a classroom full of kids work together on a project they actually cared about.

Those moments are not accidents. They are evidence of the teacher you're capable of being when you have the space and energy to show up fully.

Teachers feeling like they are "building the plane while flying it" regain purpose via collaborative check-ins, reducing isolation. Teaching is a team sport, and isolation is one of the fastest paths to burnout. When teachers have regular opportunities to share struggles, celebrate wins, and remind each other why this work matters, the shift from joy to overwhelm becomes visible before it becomes irreversible.

Low-pressure teaching – like tutoring, small-group interventions, or workshops – can recapture joy from student progress without full classroom burdens. One educator exited full-time teaching in 2019 due to burnout, then launched hands-on STEM workshops, rediscovering joy through student curiosity and laughter, free from grading and meetings. She said: "When you help children build, invent and explore ideas freely, you are reminded of why you became a teacher in the first place. It is education at its most authentic – inspiring curiosity, not ticking boxes."

Lifelong learning – enrolling in courses or professional development – triggers novelty, which releases dopamine and renews enthusiasm. This doesn't mean adding more to your plate.

It means choosing learning experiences that genuinely interest you, that remind you what it feels like to be curious, that reconnect you to the version of yourself who loves discovering new things.

Nature and mindfulness help connect with broader purpose, complemented by meditation or spiritual reading. Spiritual recovery is all about reigniting the drive and motivation. One teacher recovered by prioritizing nature time and relational reconnection, moving from isolation to renewed purpose after acknowledging burnout openly. She spent weekends hiking instead of grading. She started saying no to committees that drained her. She stopped apologizing for protecting her time. And slowly, the thread back to joy became visible again.

Build connections with colleagues and students to boost dopamine, belonging, and motivational resilience. Positive social interactions are known to increase dopamine levels. This means having real conversations, not just transactional exchanges. It means asking a colleague how they are really doing. It means sitting with a student at lunch not because you have to but because you want to. It means remembering that teaching is relational work, and relationships are what sustain us.

Seek external guidance from coaches, therapists, or peers, normalizing help as a strength. You do not have to do this alone. Asking for help is not a sign that you're failing. It's a sign that you're serious about staying in this profession for the long haul.

The thread back to passion is not about returning to who you were when you started teaching. You are not that person anymore. You've learned things. You've survived things. You have grown. The thread leads forward, not backward. It leads to a version of teaching that honors both your original why and the wisdom you've gained along the way. It leads to a career that is sustainable, fulfilling, and worth protecting. And it starts with the decision to stop drowning and start building something better.

You did not lose your passion. You buried it under too much weight. The work ahead is not about finding a new reason to teach. It's about remembering the reason you started and building a teaching life that protects it. You are not broken. You are under-equipped. And that changes now. The tools, strategies, and systems in the chapters ahead exist for one reason: to give you back the career you thought you had to sacrifice to survive. You deserve better. Your students deserve better. And it starts with recognizing that the exhaustion you feel is not a personal failure – it's a signal that something needs to change. The thread back to joy is real. And you're about to find it.

Chapter 3. Map Your Year, Own Your Year – Planning With Confidence When Life Refuses to Cooperate

What if you could walk into your classroom on the first day of school knowing exactly what you were going to teach every single week for the entire year? Not a rigid, inflexible script, but a clear roadmap that keeps you on track and eliminates the nightly panic of figuring out what comes next.

Right now, you're probably planning week by week, sometimes day by day, constantly asking yourself if you are on pace, if you've covered enough, if you're forgetting something critical. You lie awake Sunday nights mentally rehearsing Monday's lessons. You scramble during lunch to photocopy materials you just realized you need. You feel behind even when you're working ahead because you have no idea what "ahead" actually looks like.

This is not a sustainable way to teach. And it is completely unnecessary.

Year-long curriculum mapping changes the game. It's the single most powerful tool you can use to reclaim your time, reduce your stress, and teach with confidence all year long. When you map your entire year before it begins, you create a clear path forward that shows you exactly where you are going, what you need to get there, and how much time you have to make it happen. You stop reacting and start leading. You stop guessing and start knowing.

And when the inevitable happens, because snow days and flu outbreaks and emergency assemblies are not a question of if but when, you will not spiral. You will have a plan for that too.

Why Year-Long Planning Is Your Greatest Stress Reliever

A curriculum map is an overarching framework that specifies what topics, objectives, and assessments you will cover throughout the academic year and when you will cover them. Think of it as a GPS for your school year, detailing what students will learn, when they will learn it, and how it all connects to broader milestones. Learning becomes continual, sequential, integrated, and cumulative while pacing the curriculum to cover all objectives.

The primary way year-long planning relieves stress is by eliminating daily uncertainty. When you have a clear roadmap, you no longer wake up wondering what comes next or whether you're on track. You know exactly where you are in the year, what you've already covered, and what is coming up. This reduces the "what's next?" panic and builds genuine confidence in your ability to cover content at the right pace.

Teachers who use structured curriculum maps report a 42% increase in lesson planning efficiency and 40% more time saved in unit planning because they are not starting every unit from scratch. That upfront investment of time yields efficiencies that streamline preparation and balance workloads throughout the year.

Another critical benefit is the ability to measure planned instruction against actual instruction in real time. When you have a map, you can see immediately if you're falling behind or if students need more time on a particular concept, and you can make adjustments without derailing the entire year. This kind of proactive management allows you to identify student needs faster. One school using curriculum mapping provided tailored support to struggling students three weeks earlier than in prior years, alongside a 17% rise in math scores.

Year-long planning also reduces cognitive load. When you know what prerequisites students need and what content is coming next, you prevent unnecessary reteaching and clarify your responsibilities. You stop duplicating efforts, filling gaps you did not know existed, and overlapping with what other teachers have already covered. Maps enable resource sharing across units, making collaboration easier and more effective.

Technology-driven curriculum mapping platforms have been shown to enhance standards coverage by 27%, and schools using comprehensive maps report a 35% increase in instructional coherence. These improvements translate directly into less stress, more confidence, and better outcomes for both you and your students.

Year-long planning is not about adding more work to your plate. It's about doing the right work once so you do not have to keep reinventing the wheel every single week.

Building Your Annual Curriculum Map: A Step-by-Step Guide

Creating an annual curriculum map might sound overwhelming, but it's far more manageable than you think, and the payoff is immediate. A curriculum map diagrams learning objectives, activities, resources, and assessments across a course or grade level, ensuring alignment with standards, pacing, and student needs. It identifies gaps, redundancies, misalignments, and omissions while promoting coherence and flexibility.

The key is to develop your map backward from long-term desired results, avoiding the common pitfall of treating your textbook as the sole curriculum. The process breaks down into four clear steps.

Step 1: Identify Desired Results

Start by gathering inputs from standards, your own teaching experience, district philosophy, and student needs. List all content standards and curriculum expectations for your grade level or subject. Then prioritize. Identify the essential content that absolutely must be covered and what can be deprioritized if time runs short. Define your long-term goals and performance outcomes: What should students know and be able to do by the end of the year? Sequence your units logically, whether chronologically, thematically, or by building complexity.

A helpful starting point is a 90-to-120-minute brainstorming session, either alone or with your team. This focused time investment sets the foundation for the entire year.

Step 2: Determine Assessment Evidence

Once you know what you want students to learn, determine how you will know they have learned it. Align your assessments with the desired results you identified in Step 1. Select assessment types, whether formative checks, summative tests, projects, or presentations, and ensure they cover all the goals you outlined. Map the timing of these assessments to pace your instruction backward:

if students need to demonstrate mastery in March, when do you need to start teaching that content?

This step reveals whether your standards are truly being met and highlights gaps early enough to address them. It also prevents the common mistake of teaching content without ever assessing whether students actually learned it.

Step 3: Plan Learning Experiences

Now you're ready to detail how you will deliver the content. Outline the activities, resources, and differentiation strategies you will use. Sequence topics with attention to prerequisites and build in flexibility. Aim for a 20% buffer of time to accommodate reteaching, enrichment, or unexpected disruptions. Incorporate interdisciplinary links where possible to deepen learning and make connections across subjects.

Review your draft map for clarity. Flag any gaps or areas where you need additional resources. Set a timeline for revisions so the map remains a living document rather than something you create once and forget.

Step 4: Implement, Review, and Iterate

Share your map digitally so team members can edit and align across grade levels. Monitor progress mid-year using student data and adjust as needed. Use a simple template that includes units, standards, assessments, resources, and pacing. The format matters less than the clarity and usability of the information.

Real results back this up. One district's team used 90-minute sessions to draft maps, achieving 100% standards coverage and reducing teacher planning time by 30%. Another K-12 implementation produced year overviews that enabled seamless grade articulation and collaborative instruction.

Best practices include collaborating with your team, using software for real-time updates, building in 10 to 20% flexible time for disruptions, and reviewing your map annually with new data. This is not a one-and-done task. It is a tool that evolves with you and your students.

Accounting for Holidays, Testing, and the Natural Rhythms of the Year

Even the most beautifully designed curriculum map will fail if it doesn't account for the realities of the school calendar. Year-long planning means paying close attention to holidays, testing periods, and the natural rhythms of the school year to create a flexible, realistic plan that prevents overload.

The first step is identifying all non-instructional days early in the planning process: holidays, professional development days, conferences, field trips, testing windows. This allows you to calculate the actual number of teaching days you have each month, ensuring your pacing aligns with available time. This simple act transforms reactive planning into proactive strategy and eliminates the calendar surprises that throw everything off course.

A month that looks like it has 20 school days might yield only 14 or 15 actual instructional days once you subtract assemblies, testing, and field trips. Some months might have as few as four instructional contacts, making trimester or semester views more practical than monthly mapping. Your plan must allow for rerouting when disruptions like snow days compress your content delivery timeline.

Testing windows deserve special attention. Mark all required testing periods explicitly on your curriculum map and back-map review time beforehand. If your state tests are in April, you need to allocate preparation weeks in March. Required assessments, including state tests, district benchmarks, and performance tasks, shape your overall pacing and must be gathered alongside standards during initial planning. Space your assessments thoughtfully to prevent overload during high-stakes weeks. Students cannot perform well on a major project if it's due the same week as standardized testing.

Beyond holidays and testing, you need to account for the natural rhythms of the school year. The week before winter break is not the time to introduce complex new concepts. The late spring months often bring restlessness and distraction. September is full of energy but also adjustment. June is exhausting for everyone. Your curriculum map should reflect these realities.

When you account for these rhythms in your curriculum map, you create a plan that works with the school year rather than against it. You stop feeling blindsided by the calendar and start feeling prepared.

Building Buffer Zones Into Your Calendar

No matter how carefully you plan, life will happen. Students will get sick, snow will fall, fire drills will interrupt your best lesson, and assemblies will appear on your calendar with zero notice. A parent conference will run long. The technology will fail right when you need it most. And somewhere around mid-October, you will look at your beautifully mapped curriculum and realize you're already two weeks behind.

This is not a sign that you are failing. This is not evidence that your planning was pointless. This is what teaching looks like in the real world.

Buffer zones are designated extra time built into your calendar to accommodate unforeseen delays and unexpected events. Rather than scheduling lessons, grading, and administrative tasks back-to-back with no margin for error, buffer zones create breathing room that allows you to respond to disruptions without cascading stress and missed deadlines. Think of them as shock absorbers for your school year.

The most effective way to build buffer zones is to intentionally leave 15 to 20% of your available time unscheduled when planning your week. If you have five instructional days, do not plan five days of brand-new content. Plan three and a half to four days of new material, and leave the remaining time as flexible space. This doesn't mean wasted time. It means time that can be used for review, reteaching, extension activities, or catching up when something takes longer than expected.

When creating your year-long curriculum map, build in full buffer weeks at strategic points throughout the year. Place one before winter break, one before spring break, and one in late April or early May. Label these weeks as "review and enrichment" or "flex week" on your map. During these weeks, you can review key concepts, provide differentiated support, or move forward if you're genuinely on pace. But if you're behind, and you will be at some point, these weeks give you permission to catch up without guilt.

Carving out time on Friday afternoons to organize your system for the following week can make Monday mornings much less stressful. During this planning time, assess where you actually are versus where you planned to be. If you're behind, use your buffer time to adjust. If you're on track, use the buffer for enrichment or to get ahead on future prep work.

Effective buffer zone creation begins with understanding which tasks have rigid deadlines and which have flexibility. Report card comments must be submitted by a specific date. Parent-teacher conferences happen on scheduled days. But the timing of certain lessons, the order of specific activities, and the pacing within a unit often have more flexibility than you realize.

Prioritize your own wellbeing by blocking out your breaks first. You will work more efficiently when rested. Set a firm time when you stop working for the day. When that time arrives, close your laptop and disengage from work-related tasks. These boundaries are not luxuries. They are essential buffers that protect you from burnout and ensure you have the energy to adapt when disruptions occur.

Recovering Gracefully When Plans Get Disrupted

When unexpected events derail your plans, the first step is to pause and assess rather than panic. Take fifteen minutes to look at your curriculum map and identify what is truly essential versus what is nice to have. Teachers can audit curricula to eliminate low-value activities, which consume about 40% of class time, refocusing on essential skills. This is not about lowering standards. It's about hyper-critically selecting high-value lessons to maximize limited time.

Recovery starts with prioritizing high-impact instructional adjustments. If you lose three days to snow, you cannot simply pick up where you left off and expect students to remember everything. Instead, infuse movement and breaks into your first day back. Incorporate physical activity like standing to act out directions or charades for vocabulary. Short breaks restore focus and inject joy. These activities re-engage students while also giving you time to gauge where they are academically.

Reteach with targeted diagnostics rather than re-teaching everything to everyone. Sample a few students to identify misconceptions, model success with one student, then scale the reteach using their progress as an anchor. This approach saves time and targets the actual gaps rather than assuming all students need the same review.

When you return from a disruption, gather quick data to pinpoint needs, then develop a targeted instruction plan. This might be a five-question exit ticket, a quick verbal check-in, or a one-minute written response. Use this information to group students by specific skill needs rather than grade levels for targeted small-group instruction. You do not need to reteach the entire lesson to the entire class. You need to address specific gaps for specific students.

Leverage technology for personalized learning experiences when you need to catch up. Digital platforms can provide differentiated practice while you work with small groups, effectively allowing you to be in two places at once.

Communicate openly with peers, mentors, and administrators about timeline adjustments. If the entire grade level or school experienced the same disruption, work together to adjust pacing guides and share resources. You do not have to recover alone.

When adjusting your plan, reschedule less urgent activities when critical responsibilities demand attention. That creative extension project can wait. That elaborate bulletin board can be simplified. That extra enrichment activity can be cut. Protect the core content and let go of the rest without guilt.

Recovering gracefully means accepting that you will not make up every single lost minute. You will not teach every single thing you originally planned. And that is okay. The goal is to ensure students master the essential standards and finish the year having learned what matters most. Everything else is negotiable.

Making Peace With Imperfection While Staying on Track

Experienced educators recognize that mistakes are part of the joy, and the messiness is part of the humanity. A classroom is a vibrant, unpredictable place where the unexpected is woven into the fabric of each day. When you accept this reality, you stop fighting against the natural chaos of teaching and start working with it instead.

Teachers who openly admit flaws create a culture of compassion and continuous improvement. When you show your students that you are imperfect, it lets them know that their imperfections are okay too. They can struggle with a math problem, lose their train of thought, or get frustrated, and you will still care about them just as deeply.

Modeling failure in real time, owning a lesson flop, reflecting, and adjusting, normalizes risk-taking and prevents perfectionism from stifling progress. When a lesson doesn't go the way you planned, say it out loud: "That did not go the way I planned. Let me think about what we can do differently tomorrow." This transparency teaches students that setbacks are temporary and solvable, not catastrophic.

Incorporate low-stakes failure opportunities, such as board games or STEM challenges, to build student tolerance for imperfection while keeping curriculum momentum. These activities teach resilience while also giving you flexibility in your schedule. If you're behind on a unit, a board game that reinforces key concepts counts as instructional time while also providing a mental break for everyone.

Embracing imperfection doesn't mean settling for mediocrity. It means recognizing that growth comes from continuous learning and adaptation. When you make a mistake, and you will make approximately 1,500 decisions every single day, so mistakes are inevitable, reflect on what happened, adjust, and move forward. Fifteen years into teaching, experienced educators have stopped seeking that elusive perfect day when everything goes just right: the smooth pacing, the masterful sequence of questions, the firm yet forgiving demeanor. They have learned that perfect days are rare, but good-enough days are abundant when you stop demanding perfection.

Making peace with imperfection while staying on track means accepting that your year will not unfold exactly as planned, and that is not a failure. It means measuring success by whether students learned what they needed to learn, not by whether you checked off every box on your original plan.

Finishing the Year Strong Without Burning Out

Teacher burnout peaks toward year-end due to accumulated fatigue from disruptions, mounting paperwork, and the psychological weight of months of giving everything you have. The final months test every teacher's resilience. You are tired. Your students are tired. The finish line is visible but still feels impossibly far away.

This is when sustainable strategies matter most.

In the final months, protect your buffer zones fiercely. Do not let guilt convince you to fill every available minute with new content. Audit your remaining to-do list and eliminate anything that does not directly serve student learning or required compliance. That elaborate end-of-year project can be simplified. Those extra assessments can be cut. Focus on what matters and release the rest.

Set reasonable expectations and accept that plans will remain incomplete. When you feel overwhelmed, pause and take a few deep breaths before responding to the next demand. This simple practice creates space between stimulus and response, preventing reactive decisions driven by exhaustion.

Check in with yourself weekly. How am I feeling? What is my energy level? What do I need right now? Answer honestly and adjust accordingly. Prioritize sleep, restful weekends, and personal time. In the final months, this becomes non-negotiable. Go to bed earlier.

Say no to optional commitments. Protect your weekends, because they are what make it possible to keep showing up.

Talk regularly with peers for shared understanding and support. In the final months, lean on your colleagues. Share resources. Vent when you need to. Celebrate small wins together. You are not alone in this exhaustion, and connection is one of your most powerful tools for resilience.

The final weeks of school will be chaotic regardless of what you do. Field trips, assemblies, awards ceremonies, and end-of-year activities will disrupt your schedule. Students will be restless and distracted. And that is okay. Your goal is not to maintain perfect instruction until the final bell. Your goal is to cross the finish line with your sanity intact and your passion for teaching still alive.

You planned your year. You built in buffers. You recovered from disruptions. You made peace with imperfection. Staying on track was never about rigid adherence to a schedule. It was about having the resilience to keep moving forward when life happened. The year may not have unfolded exactly as you envisioned, but you made it through. Your students learned. You grew. And you protected enough of yourself to come back and do it again next year.

That is what finishing strong really means.

Chapter 4. AI 101 – What It Is, What It Isn't, and Why You Don't Need to Be Afraid

You do not need to be a tech expert to use AI in your teaching. You do not need to understand coding, algorithms, or anything remotely complicated to make AI work for you starting today.

You've been using it all along without even thinking about it. If you've ever sent an email, you have already used AI. Every time your inbox automatically filters spam, that is AI working quietly in the background. When your phone suggests the next word as you type a text message, that is AI. When Netflix recommends a show you might like, that is AI.

The difference now is that AI has become powerful enough to handle the kinds of tasks that have been stealing your evenings and weekends – lesson planning, grading, drafting emails to parents, creating assessments, and organizing materials. The technology that once felt like science fiction is now as accessible as opening a web browser.

Simply put, AI can give you back the time and energy that the profession has been taking from you for years. It is here to handle the repetitive, exhausting tasks that drain you so you can focus on the work that actually matters – the human connections, the moments of inspiration, the relationships that change lives.

What AI Actually Is (In Plain English)

Artificial intelligence sounds intimidating, but the reality is far simpler than most people realize. At its core, AI is computer software that can perform tasks that normally require human thinking – like recognizing patterns, solving problems, making decisions, and learning from experience.

That's it. No magic. No mystery. Just software that has been trained to handle specific tasks by learning from massive amounts of data.

Think of it this way: traditional computer programs are like recipes. Every single step is written out in advance, and the computer follows those instructions exactly. If the recipe says add two cups of flour, the program adds two cups of flour. It cannot adapt or improvise.

AI is different. AI is like teaching someone to cook by showing them a million examples of successful meals instead of writing out every single instruction. The AI learns what works by studying patterns across all those examples, and then it applies what it learned to new situations.

This is why AI can do things that feel almost human – like understanding what you're asking for when you type a question, or generating a lesson plan that fits your curriculum, or providing feedback on student writing. It's not actually thinking the way you think. It's recognizing patterns in language, structure, and content based on everything it has learned from its training data.

Current AI systems can understand and process human language, including both speech and written text. They can analyze enormous datasets far faster than any human could. They can generate new content – text, images, suggestions – based on patterns they have identified. They can automate repetitive tasks and help improve decision-making processes.

For teachers, this means AI can assist with grading, lesson planning, data analysis, and content generation – the exact tasks that consume hours of prep time every single week.

There are a few key technologies that make this possible, but you don't need to understand the technical details to use them.

- Machine learning is the process by which systems learn from data without being explicitly programmed for every scenario.
- Natural language processing is what allows machines to understand and work with human language – this is what powers chatbots and writing assistants.
- Generative AI is the type that creates new content based on patterns in its training data – tools like ChatGPT and Claude fall into this category.

AI is not magic, and it is not inherently dangerous. AI tools operate within the boundaries of their training data – they are software applications, not something to fear. And AI is absolutely not replacing human judgment.

Just like calculators did not eliminate mathematicians, AI will not eliminate teachers. It augments human decision-making. Teachers remain essential for the nuanced, emotionally intelligent work of education. What it will do is handle the time-consuming tasks that drain you, freeing you to inspire, mentor, and connect with your students in ways that only you can.

Separating Fact From Fear: Common Misconceptions About AI

The conversation around AI in education is full of fear, and much of that fear comes from misconceptions that exaggerate risks while overlooking the ways AI can actually support teachers. It's time to separate fact from fear so you can make informed decisions about how AI fits into your teaching practice.

Misconception: AI will replace teachers.

This is the fear that keeps many educators from even exploring AI tools, but the reality is the opposite. AI enhances teaching by automating administrative tasks, which allows you to focus on mentorship, emotional support, and the relational work that defines great teaching – areas where AI falls completely short. AI lacks contextual reasoning, ethical judgment, and emotional intelligence. It cannot read a student's body language when they are struggling. It cannot sense when a classroom needs a moment of humor or grace. It cannot build the trust that makes learning possible. A UNESCO report found that 78% of educators value AI for its ability to personalize learning without replacing the teacher. AI is a teaching assistant, not a replacement.

Misconception: AI encourages cheating.

When students use AI to complete assignments without thinking, that is a concern – but it is not an AI problem, it's a design problem. AI actually promotes critical thinking and responsible use when teachers guide students with clear policies and intentional assignments. Instead of asking students to produce work that AI can easily generate, teachers can design tasks that require students to use AI as a research tool, then apply their own analysis and creativity. This strengthens research skills rather than serving as a shortcut. The key is teaching students how to use AI ethically, just as previous generations learned to use calculators and search engines responsibly.

Misconception: AI is always accurate and unbiased.

AI can make mistakes. It can misinterpret context. It can inherit biases from its training data, which means it can sometimes amplify societal biases that disproportionately harm marginalized students. AI models can provide outdated information or generate responses that sound confident but are factually wrong. This is why human oversight is essential. You are the expert in your classroom. AI provides suggestions, drafts, and starting points – but you're the one who reviews, refines, and makes the final call. This is not a weakness of AI. It is a reminder that your judgment is irreplaceable.

Misconception: AI makes students lazy.

The opposite is often true. AI can spark innovation by offering personalized feedback and challenges that meet students exactly where they are, freeing up time for original thinking. Platforms that use AI can customize assignments to push students toward problem-solving rather than passive consumption. When students receive instant feedback on their work, they can revise and improve in real time instead of waiting days for a teacher to return graded assignments. This accelerates learning and builds independence, not laziness.

Misconception: AI is too complicated for teachers to use.

Many AI tools are designed with intuitive interfaces and come with training support, making them accessible even to educators who do not consider themselves tech-savvy. You do not need to understand how AI works under the hood any more than you need to understand how your car engine works to drive to school. The tools are built for users, not engineers. If you can type a question into Google, you can use AI.

Misconception: AI promotes a one-size-fits-all approach.

In reality, AI personalizes learning by analyzing individual student patterns and adapting content to meet diverse needs. It can adjust to different school resources, different student populations, and different teaching styles. The flexibility of AI is one of its greatest strengths, not a limitation.

Surveys show that 46% of teachers and 48% of students are already using tools like ChatGPT. The educators who are using AI are not abandoning their students – they are finding ways to work smarter so they can show up as better, more present teachers. The fear is real, but it is not based on the reality of how AI actually functions in the classroom.

AI as Your Teaching Assistant, Not Your Replacement

Imagine having a teaching assistant who never gets tired, never calls in sick, and can handle an endless list of repetitive tasks without complaint. That assistant does not take over your classroom or make decisions about your students. Instead, it handles the grading, generates draft lesson plans, organizes materials, and provides instant feedback so you can focus on the work that only you can do – mentoring, inspiring, and connecting with students on a human level. That is exactly what AI offers.

AI excels at processing vast amounts of data and generating personalized feedback, while teachers provide the nuanced guidance required for complex emotional and social issues. AI can handle procedural tasks – like building a quiz, drafting a rubric, or summarizing a text – while you oversee the bigger picture and make the decisions that require professional judgment.

The time savings alone are significant. AI can generate drafts for quizzes, rubrics, summaries, and lesson materials in minutes. One veteran teacher described it this way: "It gives me time back – time that I can spend working with kids instead of creating worksheets."

That time adds up. Instead of spending Sunday afternoon writing a new assessment from scratch, you spend twenty minutes reviewing and refining an AI-generated draft. Instead of staying late every night grading essays, you use AI to provide initial feedback and then add your own personal comments where they matter most. Sixty percent of teachers already use AI for grading and generating exercises.

AI also provides personalized support for students in ways that would be impossible for one teacher managing a classroom of twenty-five or more. Tools can adapt instruction in real time, identify learning gaps, support multilingual learners with translations, and provide instant feedback on assignments.

In one study, 77% of students using AI chatbots found them helpful for answering conceptual questions, which freed up their instructors to focus on advanced inquiries and deeper discussions. One professor put it this way: "I would love it if the bot could answer the easy questions, and then they could come to me with the hard ones."

Real-world examples show how this works in practice.

- The University of Michigan's Maizey chatbot received 77% positive feedback from students who used it for conceptual guidance.
- Squirrel Ai, which serves 24 million students, improved question accuracy from 78% to 93% by using personalized learning paths informed by data from 10 billion learning interactions.
- At George Washington University, Professor Alexa Alice Joubin customized an open-source AI tool to detect writing patterns and provide feedback to humanities students.
- In K-12 classrooms, AI has been used to support vocabulary development for elementary students, provide translations for multilingual learners, and offer essay feedback for high schoolers.

Experts are clear about the role AI should play: "AI in education supports teaching, not replacing teachers. Its impact relies on quality instruction and thoughtful use." Another educator put it simply: "What we need is a tireless teacher assistant who can take on some of the work. AI makes a perfect teacher assistant for these menial tasks."

Sean Torney, an education technology leader, noted, "AI can really be a powerful assistant. This can increase productivity and boost creativity." And perhaps most importantly: "Human teachers bring emotional intelligence... teachers serve as mentors and role models... But the real magic happens when these strengths are combined."

AI lacks emotional intelligence, contextual understanding, and the ability to foster social-emotional development – these are core teacher strengths that no technology can replicate. Concerns about accuracy, privacy, and equity are valid and require clear guidelines and professional development. But 71% of teachers view AI as essential for student success, provided it's used collaboratively rather than as a replacement.

The goal is not to hand over your classroom to a machine. But you can hand over the tasks that exhaust you so you can reclaim the parts of teaching that made you fall in love with this profession in the first place.

Why Now Is the Perfect Time to Start Using AI

If you've been hesitant to explore AI, waiting for the right moment, this is it. AI tools in 2026 are practical, user-friendly, and widely integrated into K-12 education in ways that make adoption straightforward even for teachers without technical expertise. The technology has matured. The tools are accessible. The research is clear. And the benefits are too significant to ignore.

Generative AI applications like ChatGPT can handle routine tasks such as lesson planning, quiz generation, and grading, reducing teacher workload by up to 37% and saving nearly six weeks per year for regular users. Sixty-nine percent of teachers report that AI has improved their teaching methods, with tools providing real-time adaptations, instant feedback, and personalized content creation.

These are not experimental tools anymore. They are proven solutions that thousands of educators are already using to reclaim their time and improve student outcomes.

The benefits extend beyond time savings. AI automates administrative burdens, which allows teachers to redirect their energy toward student interaction and personalized instruction. It generates drafts for rubrics, summaries, and assessments. It provides immediate feedback to students. It identifies at-risk learners early, improving retention by 15% and engagement by tenfold.

For students, AI delivers personalized learning pathways, adaptive tutoring, and equitable access – particularly for multilingual, neurodivergent, or disabled learners – yielding 54% higher test scores and 30% better outcomes in controlled trials. These gains are even more pronounced in under-resourced areas facing teacher shortages.

AI also directly addresses teacher burnout by handling the repetitive tasks that drain energy and steal personal time. One veteran teacher said it perfectly: "It gives me time back – time that I can spend working with kids instead of creating worksheets."

Fifty-three percent of K-12 districts now prioritize AI specifically for teacher support, recognizing that sustainable teaching careers depend on reducing unsustainable workloads. This is not just about productivity. It's about protecting your wellbeing so you can build a career that lasts.

Experts across the field agree. "By reducing time spent on numerous teaching-related tasks, AI allows teachers to focus on individualized student attention and enhance curriculum and instruction." Another study concluded, "What we found was that there are real benefits of generative AI for students learning when the power of AI is held back, used very narrowly, integrated with vetted content and good pedagogy."

And perhaps most compellingly: "Artificial intelligence in education is supporting teachers in working smarter by taking on activities such as grading, lesson planning, and tracking student learning to free up teachers to coach and mentor students."

The tools are ready. The research is solid. The support systems are in place. The only question left is whether you're ready to give yourself permission to work smarter instead of harder.

Chapter 5. Is AI Safe in My Classroom? Ethics, Privacy, and Responsible Use

The truth is that many teachers avoid AI altogether because they are afraid of doing something wrong. They worry about violating student privacy laws, breaking district policies they have never seen, or accidentally exposing sensitive information.

That fear is completely understandable. The stakes are high when you're responsible for the well-being and data security of dozens of children every single day.

But avoiding AI entirely is not the answer, because the right tools, used responsibly, can genuinely transform your workload and give you back the personal time you desperately need.

By the end of this chapter, you'll have a clear framework for using AI safely and ethically – one that protects your students, honors your professional integrity, and allows you to move forward with the strategies in this book without hesitation or guilt.

Understanding Student Data Privacy and FERPA Compliance

The Family Educational Rights and Privacy Act, known as FERPA, is the federal law that governs how schools handle student information. Enacted in November 1974, FERPA applies to any school receiving federal funding under a program administered by the U.S. Secretary of Education.

If your school receives federal funding – and nearly all public K-12 schools do – then FERPA applies to you. Schools that fail to comply with FERPA risk losing that federal funding, which is why districts take these regulations seriously.

FERPA establishes fundamental protections for student educational records. It grants students the right to inspect and review their education records, request corrections, halt the release of personally identifiable information, and obtain copies of access policies.

The law prohibits institutions from disclosing personally identifiable information in education records without written consent. For students under 18, parents and guardians hold these rights. When a student turns 18 or enrolls in postsecondary education, these rights transfer to the student.

The types of records protected under FERPA include grades, transcripts, disciplinary records, special education records such as IEPs, school health records, financial aid records, and test scores. Essentially, if it is part of a student's educational file and it identifies that student, FERPA protects it.

Consent is the most important requirement of FERPA. Schools cannot share identifiable information without explicit written permission from parents for students under 18 or from students themselves if they are 18 or older. Valid consent must be signed and dated, specify which records will be disclosed, state the purpose of disclosure, and identify the parties who will receive the information. Oral consent does not meet FERPA's requirements – consent must be written.

There are exceptions to the consent requirement. FERPA permits disclosure without consent to law enforcement and courts when subpoenas are issued, to authorized school officials with legitimate educational interest, and for audit or evaluation of federal or state education programs.

Schools may also release directory information such as names and addresses without consent, though families can opt out. Since 2002, high schools must provide student contact information to military recruiters unless families opt out.

Schools have specific obligations under FERPA. They must notify parents and eligible students annually of their FERPA rights. They must provide access to education records within 45 days of a request. Stakeholders may request amendments to incorrect information. Every educational agency must train employees to comply with FERPA rules, including teachers, administrative staff, IT personnel, campus security, and third-party vendors.

For teachers using AI tools, FERPA compliance requires several practical steps.

- First, any third-party AI platform that accesses student data requires written consent specifying which data will be shared, with whom, and for what purpose.
- Second, you should share only the minimum necessary student information with any tool.
- Third, maintain clear records of data sharing and authorization.
- Fourth, inform students and families about how AI tools will use their data before obtaining consent.

- Finally, work within your district's established data privacy and AI use policies, which should be aligned with FERPA.

Institutions should implement access control systems that restrict data to authorized personnel with legitimate educational interest and employ multi-factor authentication. Educational agencies must use reasonable methods to authenticate the identity of parties seeking access to records.

These technical safeguards are typically handled at the district level, but as a classroom teacher, you play a critical role in the human side of compliance – making thoughtful decisions about what information you share and with whom.

What You Should Never Share With AI Tools

AI tools in K-12 classrooms pose significant data privacy risks because the information you input may be stored, reused for training models, or exposed to breaches, violating laws like FERPA and compromising student trust. Publicly available generative AI platforms such as ChatGPT or Claude often retain user data indefinitely, potentially training future models or enabling retrieval by other users. So these tools should be treated like public forums, which means avoiding any input that could identify individuals or reveal confidential information.

Never input personally identifiable information into AI tools.

This includes names, addresses, phone numbers, Social Security numbers, identification numbers, birthdates, or family details. Even seemingly harmless details can become identifying when combined. For example, a student's first name combined with their grade level, school name, and a specific assignment topic could potentially identify that child.

Never input student records and academic data.

This includes grades, disciplinary records, attendance data, essays with personal identifiers, or any protected education records under FERPA. If you want to use AI to help you provide feedback on student writing, you must remove all identifying information first. Change the student's name to a placeholder like "Student A" or "the writer." Remove any references to specific schools, teachers, family members, or locations that appear in the essay.

Never input health and medical information.

Student health records, disabilities, mental health notes, or medical histories should never be shared with AI tools. This includes information from IEPs or 504 plans that identify specific student needs or diagnoses. If you're using AI to help differentiate instruction, describe the learning need in general terms without identifying the student or revealing protected health information.

Never input financial and HR data.

Credit card details, financial aid information, payroll, HR records, or proprietary school financials should never be entered into AI platforms. This protects both students and staff members from potential identity theft or data breaches.

Never input proprietary or confidential content.

Unpublished research, school policies under development, contracts, algorithms, internal communications, or district-specific operational data should remain confidential. Free consumer tools lack privacy guarantees and expand attack surfaces through phishing or malicious extensions.

As one expert plainly states, "Anything you paste into an AI tool may be stored or reused by the vendor. Student records, grades, and HR information may be protected by law or contract."

Another cautions, "You should never enter any data or input that is confidential or sensitive into publicly accessible generative AI tools. This includes but is not limited to individual names, physical or email addresses, identification numbers, and specific medical, HR, financial records."

The legal frameworks of FERPA and COPPA mandate strict controls on student data disclosure to third-party vendors, requiring schools to ensure AI tools are under direct institutional control. Districts must vet AI tools for data collection practices, storage duration, and third-party sharing. Without contracts, AI vendors may claim ownership of inputs, exposing data to misuse.

One education technology expert warns, "Teachers who experiment with AI could lack crucial understanding of these platforms' privacy risks, and expose personal student information. Schools are ultimately responsible for student data, according to the law."

The best practices are straightforward.

- Remove or anonymize all identifying details before inputting text into any AI tool.

- Use district-approved, education-specific tools like Khanmigo or MagicSchool, which anonymize data and block sensitive inputs.
- Implement access controls such as strong passwords and two-factor authentication, and always review AI outputs before using them.
- Train students on digital literacy and prohibit AI use for children under 13 without parental consent.
- Consult your IT or security office for approved tools, as self-hosted AI on controlled devices is safer than cloud services.

Checking Your District's AI Policies and Guidelines

As of 2026, 34 states and Puerto Rico now have official guidance or policy on the use of AI in K-12 schools, though implementation remains uneven across districts. State-level regulation has undergone dramatic transformation since 2023, shifting from exploratory pilots and high-level guidance to enforceable local policies and transparent oversight.

Ohio became the first state to require every K-12 school district to adopt a formal AI use policy – either the state model or a locally developed policy aligned with it – by July 1, 2026. Tennessee similarly mandates that each district craft and share public policies outlining how AI may and may not be used for curriculum and assignments, a requirement in place since March 2024. Schools may either use the state template or customize it to reflect local needs, allowing flexibility while ensuring baseline expectations are met.

This means your district may have specific policies in place that govern how you can and cannot use AI tools in your classroom. Your first step is to find out whether your district has an AI use policy. Start by checking your district's website, looking in sections related to technology, acceptable use policies, or instructional guidelines.

If you cannot find a policy posted publicly, reach out to your building principal, instructional technology coordinator, or district IT department. Ask directly: "Does our district have a policy on AI use for teachers and students? If so, where can I access it?"

If your district does have a policy, read it carefully. Effective AI policies for K-12 schools need to be structured to meet existing policies about acceptable use, aligned with district goals, supported by training and transparent communication, tested with a pilot group, and improved upon continuously. Look for the following core components in your district's policy.

Data privacy and security should be addressed, including compliance with FERPA, protections for personally identifiable information, and alignment with state and federal laws. Tools should process data in a secure, transparent, and ethical manner. Your policy should clarify which AI tools have been vetted and approved for use and which have not.

Academic integrity and educator authority should be clearly defined. A strong policy guarantees that grading and discipline always come from a teacher, never an AI. AI should be a tool to support learning and teaching, not a substitute for student effort or the role of the educator. This protects your professional judgment and ensures that students understand the limits of AI assistance.

Your policy should specify that staff use only district-approved AI solutions. This protects against shadow IT threats, which occur when teachers or students use unapproved tools that have not been vetted for data security. If you want to try a new AI tool that is not on the approved list, your policy should outline the process for requesting evaluation and approval.

Safeguards for younger students should be included, with protections aligned with COPPA and regulations protecting students' identities online. This is especially important for elementary teachers working with students under 13.

Many districts are forming governance structures to oversee AI implementation. School IT teams may partner with a cross-functional team of educators and staff to determine the opportunities and obstacles to implementing AI solutions. The work group should include educators who are representative of grade levels and departments, including special education and related services professionals, along with board members, students, and external partners such as local businesses and postsecondary institutions. The group is expected to regularly review new research and guidance and provide ongoing feedback to the district.

If your district is forming such a workgroup, consider volunteering or nominating a colleague. Teacher voice is essential in shaping policies that are practical and supportive rather than overly restrictive or disconnected from classroom realities.

Community and family engagement is another important component. Parents and community members should be informed through ongoing engagement about the skills students need for the future workforce and how AI is being used in the classroom.

Districts may provide resources on the potential risks associated with the unsupervised use of AI tools. Input from community members, district employees, students, families, and professionals should inform policy development.

If your district does not yet have an AI policy, that doesn't mean you can't use AI tools. It means you need to proceed with extra caution and advocate for policy development. Reach out to your administration and suggest that the district develop clear guidelines.

In the meantime, follow the principles outlined in this chapter: never share personally identifiable student information, use only reputable tools designed for education, and be transparent with students and families about how you're using AI.

Modeling Responsible AI Use for Your Students

Modeling responsible AI use involves demonstrating ethical, transparent, and purposeful AI integration to guide students toward critical thinking, data privacy awareness, and integrity. This shifts the conversation from prohibition to education, fostering AI literacy while aligning with educational goals. Teachers build student trust and reduce misuse like plagiarism through structured activities and clear policies.

The first principle is to connect AI use directly to explicit educational purposes. Every time you use AI in your classroom, students should understand why and how it supports their learning objectives.

For example, if you're using AI to provide feedback on student writing, explain that the tool can offer suggestions quickly, but the student must evaluate those suggestions critically and make their own decisions about revision. If you're using AI to generate discussion prompts for a Socratic seminar, show students the prompts and discuss how AI can help structure conversations but cannot replace human insight and debate.

Compliance with privacy and safety is non-negotiable. Before implementing any AI tool with students, make sure you understand and can enforce data security, student privacy, and ownership rules. This means using only district-approved tools and never asking students to input personally identifiable information into AI platforms.

AI literacy and transparency are essential. Teachers should possess foundational knowledge of AI capabilities and limitations and disclose its role in assignments or feedback. If you use AI to help draft a rubric, tell your students. If you use AI to generate example sentences for a grammar lesson, share that with the class. This transparency models honesty and helps students understand that AI is a tool, not a shortcut or a secret.

Human oversight must always remain in place. Review every AI-generated resource before sharing it with students. Check for accuracy, bias, and appropriateness. Never allow AI to make decisions about student grades, discipline, or placement without your direct involvement and judgment.

Thoughtful assignment design can also reduce misuse. Chunk projects with peer feedback and position AI as a writing coach to encourage authentic work. Develop class-specific AI policies, such as requiring students to cite AI when they use it for brainstorming, and update your syllabus accordingly.

One verified success story comes from a high school English teacher who paused curriculum in March 2023 to teach AI responsibility over one week. Students explored feedback quality, bias detection, ethics, and drafted a school plagiarism policy.

The results were striking: fewer AI plagiarism cases, students proactively asking questions about appropriate use, and no claims of ignorance when issues arose.

This teacher did not avoid AI or try to ban it. Instead, she taught students how to use it responsibly, and that education made all the difference.

As one expert explains, "Teachers, students and AI can coexist – and even be effective together – with education, transparency, ethical boundaries and purpose." Another emphasizes, "With AI becoming a powerful tool in education, it's not just about knowing how to use it, but when and why to use it in ethical ways."

The evidence shows that modeling reduces discipline issues. In 2022-2023, 48 percent of teachers confronted students for AI use, a figure that rose 15 points the following year. But in classrooms where teachers model responsible use and educate students about boundaries, plagiarism decreases and ethical awareness increases.

To implement these strategies, start with short lessons. A 20-minute unit on AI do's and don'ts can set the tone for the entire year. Document your AI decisions and conduct ethics reviews as part of your planning process. Integrate AI literacy with digital citizenship curricula for ongoing reinforcement. When students see you using AI thoughtfully, transparently, and ethically, they learn to do the same.

These are not abstract principles. They are practical guidelines that protect your students, honor your professional integrity, and allow you to move forward with confidence. The concerns you have are valid, and now they have been addressed. You are ready to use AI responsibly, and that readiness is what makes everything else in this book possible.

Chapter 6. AI in Action – Your Step-by-Step Guide to Automating the Tasks That Are Stealing Your Life

You've already learned what AI is, what it is not, and how to use it responsibly. Now it's time to actually use it.

This chapter is the one you've been waiting for – the practical, roll-up-your-sleeves guide that takes you from "I know AI exists" to "I just saved three hours this week and I am never going back."

Every section that follows is built around real tasks that real teachers do every single week – tasks that drain your energy, steal your evenings, and pile up faster than you can get through them. Lesson plans. Permission slips. Parent emails. Rubrics. Substitute folders. Student feedback. All of it. And all of it can be made dramatically easier, faster, and less exhausting with the help of AI.

This chapter is organized into three parts.

- First, you will get a comprehensive list of every teaching task that AI can realistically help with – and you will probably be surprised by how many there are.
- Second, you will get a practical guide for evaluating and finding AI tools on your own, because the landscape changes so quickly that any specific recommendation made today may look different by next year.

- Third, you will get a snapshot of the best tools available as of this writing, organized by the tasks they do best, so you can start immediately.

By the end of this chapter, you will know exactly what to automate, how to find the tools to automate it, and which tools to try first.

Let's get to work.

Part One: Everything AI Can Do for You – A Complete Task Inventory

Most teachers who are new to AI underestimate it. They assume it can write lesson plans, maybe answer a few questions, and that is about it. The reality is that AI can meaningfully assist with nearly every category of work that teachers do outside of direct student instruction.

The following list is not exhaustive – AI capabilities are expanding constantly – but it represents the full scope of what is possible right now, organized by the type of work involved.

Lesson Planning and Curriculum Design

This is where most teachers start with AI, and for good reason – lesson planning is one of the single biggest time drains in the profession. Here is what AI can realistically do for you in this category:

- Generate complete lesson plan drafts from a single prompt, including objectives, activities, materials, and assessments
- Create unit plans aligned to specific state or national standards, including pacing guides

- Suggest hands-on activities, project-based learning ideas, and discussion questions for any topic
- Write essential questions, learning targets, and "I can" statements for any lesson or unit
- Generate bellringer activities, exit tickets, and transition activities
- Build differentiated versions of the same lesson for varying reading levels or learning needs
- Create vocabulary lists, word walls, and pre-teaching materials for new units
- Suggest cross-curricular connections and interdisciplinary project ideas
- Generate real-world application ideas that connect academic content to students' everyday lives
- Adapt existing lessons for different grade levels, above or below your current grade

Differentiation and Accommodation

One of the most time-consuming parts of modern teaching is meeting the diverse needs of every student in the room. AI can dramatically reduce the time this takes without reducing the quality of support you provide.

- Rewrite any text passage at a lower or higher Lexile level while preserving the core content
- Generate scaffolded versions of assignments with sentence frames, graphic organizers, or partially completed examples

- Create accommodated versions of assessments for students with IEPs or 504 plans, including modified instructions, reduced answer choices, or chunked tasks
- Write simplified directions for English Language Learners (ELLs), with key vocabulary highlighted
- Generate visual supports, anchor charts, and step-by-step reference guides for complex procedures
- Create tiered assignments that allow students to demonstrate mastery at different levels
- Suggest enrichment extensions for students who finish early or need additional challenge
- Draft language for co-teaching lesson plans and parallel instruction models

Assessment Creation

Creating high-quality assessments from scratch is one of the most time-intensive things teachers do. AI can handle the bulk of the creation so that your energy goes toward reviewing and refining, not building from zero.

- Generate multiple-choice questions at various Bloom's Taxonomy levels for any topic or text
- Create short-answer and extended-response prompts aligned to specific standards
- Write true/false, matching, fill-in-the-blank, and constructed-response items
- Build complete test and quiz documents with answer keys

- Generate alternative versions of the same assessment for retakes or testing accommodations
- Create performance-based assessment tasks, including project rubrics and scoring guides
- Write benchmark and formative assessment items aligned to your curriculum map
- Generate student self-assessment reflection prompts and peer review forms

Grading Assistance and Feedback

Grading is where teacher time goes to disappear. While AI cannot replace your professional judgment, it can dramatically accelerate the process and help you provide more meaningful feedback with less effort.

- Generate detailed written rubrics with clear descriptors for each performance level
- Create single-point rubrics and checklist-style grading tools for faster assessment
- Draft personalized written feedback for student essays based on your notes or the rubric criteria
- Generate a bank of feedback phrases organized by category – organization, evidence, mechanics, argument – that you can copy and customize
- Summarize patterns from student work so you can identify class-wide gaps without reading every paper before planning your next lesson
- Generate re-teaching suggestions based on assessment results you describe

- Write student-friendly explanations of grades and scoring decisions for parent conferences

Parent and Family Communication

Parent communication is emotionally demanding and time-consuming. AI cannot replace the relationship, but it can remove the blank-page problem that makes every email take longer than it should.

- Draft routine parent emails including weekly updates, upcoming event reminders, and homework alerts
- Write individual parent emails for sensitive situations – struggling students, behavior concerns, missing work – in a professional, compassionate tone
- Generate permission slips, field trip forms, and consent forms for any event or activity
- Create parent-friendly explanations of upcoming units, assessments, or curriculum changes
- Write newsletter content, classroom blog posts, and Class Dojo or Seesaw updates
- Draft thank-you notes to parent volunteers, donors, or community partners
- Generate FAQ documents about classroom policies, grading systems, and homework expectations
- Translate basic communications into other languages using AI translation features
- Write scripts for parent-teacher conference conversations, including how to frame difficult news supportively

- Draft responses to challenging or heated parent emails, giving you a calm, professional starting point before you edit

Administrative and Organizational Tasks

The administrative weight of teaching – paperwork, documentation, organizational systems – is one of the least visible and most exhausting parts of the job. AI can take a significant chunk of this burden off your plate.

- Create substitute teacher folders including detailed daily schedules, classroom procedures, and emergency contact information
- Generate supply lists for projects, labs, and units
- Write professional development reflection documents and goal-setting statements
- Draft responses to administrative requests, committee assignments, and professional correspondence
- Create student behavior documentation templates and incident report scaffolds
- Generate data tracking spreadsheets and progress monitoring templates
- Write professional learning community (PLC) agendas and meeting summaries
- Draft proposals for grants, classroom funding requests, or DonorsChoose projects
- Create classroom procedures, routines, and rule explanations in student-friendly language

- Build end-of-year reflection templates, portfolio structures, and transition documents for next year's teacher

Student Engagement and Enrichment

AI can help you build the kinds of engaging, creative learning experiences that drew you to teaching in the first place – without spending hours designing them from scratch.

- Generate creative writing prompts, journaling topics, and discussion questions tailored to your content
- Create escape room puzzles, scavenger hunts, and gamified review activities for any unit
- Write choice board menus that allow students to demonstrate learning in multiple ways
- Generate debate topics, Socratic seminar questions, and philosophical discussion prompts
- Create digital choice activities and hyperdoc structures for independent or station work
- Write book club discussion guides, literature circle role sheets, and reading response prompts
- Generate STEM challenge scenarios and project-based learning driving questions
- Build whole-class community-building activities and social-emotional learning discussion prompts

Professional Growth and Reflection

AI can also support your growth as a professional, helping you think more clearly and communicate more effectively about your own practice.

- Generate reflection prompts for post-lesson analysis and professional journaling
- Help you draft professional development goals, instructional coach notes, and observation preparation
- Summarize research articles and professional books into accessible takeaways
- Generate discussion questions for professional book studies and team meetings
- Help you articulate your teaching philosophy for evaluations, job applications, or national board certification
- Draft responses to observation feedback in a reflective, professional tone

Part Two: How to Find AI Tools That Work for You – An Evergreen Evaluation Guide

AI tools change fast. Platforms launch, improve, get acquired, pivot, raise prices, and sometimes disappear entirely. Any specific tool that is the gold standard today may look completely different in six months. So this section is not just a list of tools; it's a framework for thinking about and evaluating AI tools so that no matter what the landscape looks like when you read this, you will know exactly how to find what you need.

Think of this as your AI shopping guide. Use it every time you are looking for a new tool, whether you're reading this the month it was published or three years from now.

Step 1: Start With the Task, Not the Tool

The single biggest mistake teachers make when exploring AI is starting with the tool and then trying to figure out what it does. This approach leads to overwhelm, wasted time, and the feeling that AI is more complicated than it's worth.

Instead, always start with a specific problem you want to solve. Before you open a single browser tab, answer these questions:

- What specific task am I trying to make faster or easier?
- How much time does this task currently take me?
- What would a good outcome look like? (a draft I edit, a finished product, a set of options to choose from?)
- How often do I need to do this task?

The clearer you are about the task, the easier it is to evaluate whether any given tool actually solves your problem. "I want AI" is not a useful starting point. "I want to stop spending 90 minutes every Sunday writing lesson plans" is a problem AI can solve – and once you know the problem, you can find the tool.

Step 2: Know the Categories of AI Tools Available to Educators

AI tools for teachers generally fall into several distinct categories. Knowing the categories helps you search more effectively and compare tools fairly.

- **Large language model tools** (like ChatGPT, Claude, Gemini, or Microsoft Copilot) can help with almost any writing, planning, or brainstorming task. They require you to write good prompts but offer tremendous flexibility. These are often the best starting point for teachers who want maximum versatility.

- **Tools built specifically for teachers** have pre-built templates, educator-friendly interfaces, and features designed around the tasks teachers actually do. They're often less flexible than general AI tools but faster to use because you do not have to craft your own prompts from scratch. Look for platforms described as "AI for teachers" or "teacher productivity AI."

- Some tools even focus specifically on **generating, analyzing, or grading assessments**. They typically integrate with existing learning management systems (LMS) and may offer automatic scoring for certain question types.

- Some tools focus specifically on **streamlining parent and family communication**, translating messages, or managing outreach at scale.

- There are platforms that specialize in **adapting texts to different reading levels,** generating scaffolded materials, and producing differentiated versions of content.

- And there are tools **generate or curate instructional resources** – videos, activities, slide decks, readings – using AI to match your standards, grade level, and topic.

Step 3: Evaluate Any Tool Using These Seven Questions

Whenever you're considering a new AI tool, run it through this checklist before you invest time learning it or money subscribing to it.

Question 1: Does it do what I need it to do?

This sounds obvious, but many tools advertise capabilities that are vague or limited in practice. Before committing, try it on a real task you actually need to complete. Do not test it with a sample prompt – test it with your actual lesson, your actual grade level, your actual content. If the output requires so much editing that it saves you no time, it's not the right tool.

Question 2: Is student data protected?

Review the tool's privacy policy before you enter any information about your students. Look for these specific things: Does the tool have a FERPA compliance statement? Does it have a COPPA compliance statement if you teach students under 13? Does it use student data to train its AI model? Has your district approved or reviewed this tool? If you cannot find clear answers to these questions on the tool's website, do not use it with student information until you consult your school's technology or compliance team. Chapter 5 of this book covers this in depth – refer back to it if you need a refresher.

Question 3: What is the actual cost?

Many AI tools offer a free tier and a paid tier. Before you get attached to a tool, understand what the free tier actually gives you. How many uses per day or month? Does the free version produce meaningfully different quality than the paid version? Is there a district or school pricing option that might be available to you? Is there a free trial of the paid tier so you can evaluate it fully before deciding?

Question 4: How steep is the learning curve?

You do not have time to spend ten hours learning a new tool before it saves you any time. A good AI tool for teachers should produce useful results within your first or second attempt. If you find yourself watching long tutorial videos, consulting extensive documentation, or feeling more confused after trying it than before, it's not the right tool for you right now – even if it is technically excellent.

Question 5: Does it integrate with what I already use?

The best AI tool in the world creates friction if you have to completely change your workflow to use it. Before adopting a tool, check whether it connects to the systems you already rely on: your LMS (Google Classroom, Canvas, Schoology, etc.), your communication platform (email, Class Dojo, Seesaw), and your document tools (Google Docs, Microsoft Word). Integration is not required, but it dramatically reduces the time cost of adding a new tool.

Question 6: What do other teachers say?

One of the fastest ways to evaluate an AI tool is to look at what actual teachers say about it – not on the company's website, but in real communities. Educator Facebook groups, Reddit communities like r/Teachers, X (formerly Twitter) under hashtags like #EduTwitter or #AIinEducation, and platforms like Teachers Pay Teachers all have real teachers sharing honest reviews and workflows. Searching the tool's name alongside the word "review" or "honest review" often surfaces useful, unsponsored perspectives.

Question 7: Is this tool likely to still exist and function well in six months?

This is harder to evaluate, but worth considering. AI tools backed by well-established companies (including major tech companies or education-specific companies with significant funding and user bases) are more stable than brand-new startups with no track record. This doesn't mean new tools are bad – some of the most innovative options are newer – but it does mean you should be cautious about investing significant time learning a tool that might pivot or shut down before you can recoup that investment.

Step 4: Use Smart Search Strategies to Find New Tools

When you're actively looking for AI tools, the way you search matters. Here are the most effective strategies for finding quality options:

Search with educator-specific language.

Instead of searching for "AI writing tool," search for "AI lesson planning tool for teachers," "AI tool for creating rubrics," or "AI for parent communication teachers." Adding "for teachers," "K-12," or "educators" to your searches filters out tools built for other audiences and surfaces options designed with your specific needs in mind.

Look for curated educator lists.

Organizations like ISTE (International Society for Technology in Education), Common Sense Education, and Edutopia regularly publish updated roundups of recommended AI tools for educators. These lists are reviewed by educators and education technology specialists, which means they tend to highlight tools that are appropriate for classroom use, not just technically impressive. Search for these sources by name and look for their most recent publications.

Follow educators who test and review AI tools.

There is a growing community of educator-influencers and education technology specialists who test AI tools and share honest reviews. Following even a few of these voices on YouTube, LinkedIn, Instagram, or X will give you a steady stream of tool recommendations filtered through an educator's lens. Look for educators who share their actual workflows, not just promotional content.

Check your district's approved tool list first.

Before you find a tool you love and then discover it is not approved for use in your school, check whether your district has a pre-approved list of educational technology tools. Many districts have vetted certain platforms for privacy compliance and already have licenses or agreements in place. Starting with approved tools means less friction, faster adoption, and no privacy concerns.

Subscribe to one or two education technology newsletters.

Several well-regarded newsletters publish regular roundups of new AI tools for educators, including honest assessments of what works and what does not. A five-minute newsletter scan once a week keeps you informed without requiring you to actively search. Look for newsletters from established education technology organizations, university education programs, or trusted individual educators who specialize in technology integration.

Step 5: Adopt New Tools Strategically – One at a Time

The biggest mistake teachers make after discovering AI tools is trying to adopt five of them at once. This creates the exact kind of overwhelm that drove you to look for solutions in the first place.

Instead, follow this adoption sequence:

1. Choose one specific task you want to improve, using the criteria from Step 1.
2. Identify one tool that addresses that specific task, using the evaluation questions from Step 3.

3. Use that tool exclusively for two to four weeks before adding anything new.

4. Once the first tool feels genuinely automatic – you reach for it without thinking – add the next one.

Keep a simple running list (even just a sticky note or a notes app entry) of tools you want to try eventually, so you're not holding them in your head while you focus on the current one.

Part Three: AI Tools Worth Trying – A Current Snapshot

The following list reflects the AI tool landscape as of this writing in 2026. The education technology space evolves quickly. Some tools on this list may have changed significantly, merged with other platforms, updated their pricing, or added features that make them even more useful than described here. Use this section as a starting point, and apply the evaluation framework from Part Two to verify that any tool still meets your needs at the time you read this.

Tools are organized by the primary task they help with. Many tools appear in only one category even if they overlap, because the best way to approach this list is by starting with your specific need.

For Lesson Planning and Curriculum Design

One of the most widely used AI platforms built specifically for educators, **MagicSchool** offers more than 60 educator-specific tools including lesson plan generators, unit plan builders, differentiated materials, and accommodation supports. The free tier is genuinely useful. It's been adopted by many districts and is widely regarded as one of the most teacher-friendly platforms available. It doesn't require strong prompting skills because it guides you through structured inputs. A strong first choice for teachers new to AI. (magicschool.ai)

Built specifically for differentiation, **Diffit** takes any topic, article, or YouTube video and instantly generates reading-level-appropriate materials including summarized texts, vocabulary lists, comprehension questions, and multiple-choice assessments. Particularly powerful for teachers working with ELL students or students reading below grade level. The free version is functional and useful. (diffit.me)

An AI platform designed for both teachers and students, **SchoolAI** offers lesson planning tools, student AI companions with built-in guardrails, and teacher dashboards that show how students are interacting with AI. A good option for teachers who want to introduce students to AI in a controlled environment while also improving their own planning workflow. (schoolai.com)

ChatGPT, the original general-purpose AI assistant, remains one of the most versatile options available. While it requires more prompting skill than education-specific platforms, it can handle virtually any writing, planning, or brainstorming task a teacher might need. The free version (GPT-4o as of this writing) is capable and accessible. Teachers who take time to learn effective prompting find it one of the most flexible tools in their toolkit. See the sidebar at the end of this chapter for basic prompting guidance. (chat.openai.com)

Anthropic's AI assistant, **Claude**, is widely praised for producing thoughtful, nuanced writing and following complex instructions. It excels at generating curriculum-aligned lesson plans, writing parent communications with the right tone, and helping teachers think through differentiation strategies. The free version is available without an account, and the interface is clean and accessible. Like ChatGPT, it requires some prompting skill but rewards that investment with high-quality results. (claude.ai)

For Assessment and Grading

Khan Academy's AI tutor and teacher assistant offers a range of tools for generating quiz questions, providing student feedback, and supporting personalized learning. Particularly strong for math and science, and well-regarded for its pedagogical approach. Free for teachers through certain programs. (khanacademy.org/khan-labs)

Gradescope is an AI-assisted grading platform that allows teachers to grade student work more efficiently using AI grouping, rubric application, and analytics. Particularly useful for higher volume assignments and math-heavy assessments. Widely used in higher education but increasingly available for K-12. (gradescope.com)

Quizalize is an assessment platform with built-in AI features for generating quiz content and tracking student mastery data. More accessible than Gradescope for elementary and middle school teachers. (quizalize.com)

Eduaide.Ai is a comprehensive AI teaching assistant that generates assessments, rubrics, lesson plans, and feedback structures. The interface is built specifically for educators and requires minimal prompting skill. Strong for creating standards-aligned assessment materials quickly. (eduaide.ai)

For Differentiation and Accommodation

Diffit is particularly powerful here – its ability to instantly generate reading-level-appropriate texts on any topic is one of the most useful differentiating capabilities available to teachers today. (diffit.me)

A long-trusted source for differentiated reading passages, **ReadWorks AI** has integrated AI tools to generate new content and support comprehension across reading levels. Particularly strong for elementary and middle school teachers. (readworks.org)

MagicSchool's accommodation and modification tools, including its IEP accommodation generator and ELL support features, make it one of the strongest options for differentiation. (magicschool.ai)

For Parent and Family Communication

Both general-purpose AI assistants (**ChatGPT and Claude**) excel at drafting parent emails in any tone needed – from routine weekly updates to sensitive conversations about student struggles. Simply describe the situation and the tone you want, and the AI will generate a professional draft you can personalize and send. These tools handle communication tasks with a flexibility that education-specific platforms often cannot match.

A family communication platform with AI-assisted features for generating updates and sharing student work with families,

Seesaw is widely used in elementary schools and well-regarded for its parent-friendly interface. (web.seesaw.me)

Bloomz is a communication platform with built-in translation and messaging tools that allow teachers to communicate with families in multiple languages. It's increasingly integrating AI for message suggestions and communication templates. (bloomz.net)

For Substitute Folders and Administrative Tasks

MagicSchool offers a specific sub-plan generator that creates complete, detailed substitute teacher plans from your basic input. One of the most genuinely time-saving single tools on this list for a task that most teachers dread. (magicschool.ai)

ChatGPT or Claude can generate detailed substitute folders, classroom procedure documents, emergency contact templates, and administrative correspondence quickly and reliably. Describe what you need, include relevant details, and you will have a professional draft within seconds.

For teachers who already use **Notion** as an organizational platform, Notion's built-in AI features can help generate and organize administrative documents, meeting notes, planning templates, and more, all within a single workspace. (notion.so)

For Student Engagement and Creative Activities

Canva's AI tools allow teachers to generate visual materials, slide decks, graphic organizers, and creative classroom resources with minimal design skill. The education version is free for teachers and includes a growing suite of AI features. (canva.com)

BookCreator is an AI-integrated platform for creating digital books and student publishing projects. The AI features assist students and teachers in generating content, supporting ELL students, and building multimedia projects. (bookcreator.com)

The choice board generator, debate preparation tool, and engagement activity generators within **MagicSchool** are among the most useful for building student engagement activities quickly. (magicschool.ai)

For Professional Growth and Reflection

Claude and ChatGPT are excellent thinking partners for professional reflection. Ask them to prompt you with post-lesson reflection questions, help you articulate your teaching philosophy, summarize a research article you paste in, or draft professional development goals based on your current challenges. They function essentially as a thoughtful professional coach available at any hour.

Perplexity AI is a research-focused AI assistant that can summarize current educational research, answer questions about teaching strategies with citations, and help you stay current with trends in education technology. Useful for PD preparation and professional inquiry. (perplexity.ai)

Quick Start: Five Prompts to Try This Week

If you're not sure where to begin, start here. These five prompts can be typed directly into ChatGPT, Claude, or any general-purpose AI assistant and will produce immediately useful results. You do not need to be an expert. Just copy, customize the details in brackets, and send.

Prompt 1 – Lesson Plan Draft:

- "Write a detailed lesson plan for a [grade level] [subject] class on [topic]. The lesson should take [length of time] and align to [standard or objective]. Include a warm-up activity, direct instruction component, guided practice, and an exit ticket."

Prompt 2 – Permission Slip:

- "Write a professional parent permission slip for a [grade level] class field trip to [location] on [date]. The trip will involve [brief description of activities]. Include a section for parent signature, emergency contact information, and any medical or dietary considerations. Keep the tone friendly and clear."

Prompt 3 – Differentiated Materials:

- "Rewrite the following passage at a [3rd grade / 5th grade / etc.] reading level while keeping the key information accurate and engaging. Then generate five comprehension questions at different levels of Bloom's Taxonomy. Here is the original passage: [paste your text]"

Prompt 4 – Parent Email for a Difficult Conversation:

- "Draft a professional, compassionate parent email informing a family that their child [brief description of concern: is struggling with missing work / had a behavioral incident / is falling behind in reading]. The tone should be warm, solution-focused, and non-accusatory. Suggest one next step, such as a phone call or conference."

Prompt 5 – Substitute Folder:

- "Generate a detailed substitute teacher folder for a [grade level] [subject] class. Include a daily schedule, classroom rules and procedures, seating information, the lesson for the day [describe the topic briefly], emergency procedures, and a note about which students may need extra support. Make it easy for someone unfamiliar with the class to follow."

Chapter 7. Confidence in the Classroom – Owning Your Expertise and Trusting Yourself

Every teacher has a voice in their head that whispers they are not doing enough. It shows up when you leave school at a reasonable hour, when you say no to an extra committee, when you use a resource someone else created instead of making your own from scratch. It tells you that other teachers are doing more, doing better, doing it all without breaking a sweat. It compares your messy reality to everyone else's highlight reel and finds you lacking every single time.

That voice is not telling you the truth. But it is loud, persistent, and incredibly convincing.

Confidence in teaching doesn't come from being perfect and working yourself into exhaustion to prove you care enough. Real confidence comes from owning what you know, trusting your instincts, and defining success in ways that actually matter.

This chapter is about silencing that critical voice, stepping into your expertise even when you do not feel expert, and building the kind of confidence that sustains you for the long haul.

Silencing the Inner Critic and Overcoming Imposter Syndrome

Your inner critic tells you that you should have handled that situation differently, that you should be further along by now, that you should be doing more. It replays your mistakes on a loop and conveniently forgets every moment you got it right. It holds you to a standard that no human being could possibly meet and then punishes you for falling short.

Imposter syndrome is the belief that you've somehow fooled everyone into thinking you're competent when you secretly know you're not. It affects teachers at every stage of their career, but it hits especially hard in those early to mid-career years when you're expected to know what you're doing but still feel like you're figuring it out.

Here is what you need to understand: every teacher is making it up as they go along to some degree. It's a profession that requires constant adaptation, improvisation, and decision-making in real time. The teacher down the hall who looks like she has it all together is also making mistakes. She is also lying awake at night replaying a conversation with a student or a parent and wishing she had said something different.

The difference between a teacher who is paralyzed by imposter syndrome and one who moves forward with confidence is not competence. It is perspective. Confident teachers have learned to recognize the inner critic for what it is: a liar with a loud voice. They have learned to separate their worth from their worst moments and to measure their growth over time rather than against an impossible standard.

Start by naming the voice. When you catch yourself thinking "I am terrible at this" or "I have no idea what I am doing," ask yourself: Is this actually true, or is this my fear talking? What evidence do I have that contradicts this thought? If a colleague said this about themselves, what would I tell them?

You would never speak to another teacher the way your inner critic speaks to you. Extend yourself the same grace you would offer someone else.

Replace the critic's absolutes with more accurate statements. Instead of "I am terrible at classroom management," try "I'm still learning classroom management, and I am better at it than I was last year." Instead of "I should have known how to handle that situation," try "That was a new situation, and I did the best I could with the information I had."

Imposter syndrome thrives in isolation. It convinces you that you're the only one struggling, the only one who doesn't have it all figured out. So talk to other teachers about the moments you feel like a fraud. You will discover that they feel it too. Share your mistakes and your uncertainties. You'll find that honesty builds trust and community in ways that pretending to be perfect never will.

Keep a record of your wins! Create a folder in your email or a note on your phone where you save positive feedback from students, parents, and colleagues. On the hard days when the critic is especially loud, pull out that folder and remind yourself of the truth: you are making a difference, you are growing, and you are enough.

Owning Your Expertise Even When You Don't Feel Like An Expert

One of the most damaging myths in education is that good teachers never admit they do not know something. This myth keeps teachers trapped in a cycle of pretending, performing, and panicking when a student asks a question they can't answer.

The truth is that the best teachers are the ones who model lifelong learning by saying "I don't know, but let's find out together."

Owning your expertise means recognizing what you do know and being honest about what you do not. It means trusting that your years of training, your classroom experience, and your deep knowledge of your students give you a perspective that matters. You may not have all the answers, but you have enough to guide your students forward.

Expertise grows through practice, reflection, and feedback. Every lesson you teach gives you data about what works and what does not. Every interaction with a student teaches you something about how kids learn and what they need. Every mistake you make and reflect on makes you a better teacher the next time you face a similar situation.

Stop waiting to feel like an expert before you act like one. You will never wake up one morning and suddenly feel like you've arrived. Expertise is not a destination. It's a process. You are an expert in progress, and that is exactly what you're supposed to be.

Trust your instincts. You have been in your classroom long enough to develop a sense of what your students need, what works with your particular group, and what feels right for you as a teacher. When a new initiative or strategy is introduced and something in your gut says, "this is not going to work for my kids," listen to that instinct. You know your students better than any outside expert does. You are a professional making informed decisions based on your knowledge and experience.

Own your voice in professional conversations. When you're in a team meeting or a professional development session, speak up.

Share what is working in your classroom. Ask questions when something doesn't make sense. Push back when a strategy doesn't fit your students' needs. Your perspective matters, and the more you use your voice, the more confident you will become in your expertise.

Defining Success Beyond Test Scores and Evaluations

Test scores and evaluation ratings are not measures of your worth as a teacher. They are data points that reflect a narrow slice of what happens in your classroom on a particular day under particular conditions.

- They do not capture the relationship you built with the student who hated school until they walked into your room.
- They do not measure the confidence you helped a struggling reader develop or the curiosity you sparked in a kid who thought learning was boring.
- They do not account for the trauma your students are carrying, the resources your school lacks, or the hundred variables outside your control that affect student performance.

If you measure your success solely by test scores and evaluations, you will spend your career chasing a moving target and feeling like you are never quite good enough. You need a different measure of success that sustains you through the hard years and helps you recognize your impact even when the data does not show it.

Start by identifying what success looks like to you. Not to your administration, not to the state, not to the teacher down the hall who seems to have it all together. To you.

What are the moments in your classroom that make you think "this is why I teach?" What are the changes you see in your students over the course of a year that matter most? What are the skills, habits, and qualities you hope your students carry with them long after they leave your classroom?

Maybe success is the student who started the year refusing to participate and ended it raising their hand every day. Maybe it's the class discussion that went deeper than you expected because your students felt safe enough to share their real thoughts. Maybe it's the parent email that said, "my child actually likes school this year." Maybe it's the moment you realized you handled a difficult situation with more patience and skill than you would have a year ago.

These moments are not measurable by standardized tests, but they are absolutely measurable by you. Create a system for noticing and recording them. Keep a journal where you write down one success from each day, no matter how small. Take photos of student work that shows growth. Save the notes and emails that remind you of your impact. On the hard days, this record becomes evidence that you are making a difference even when it doesn't feel like it.

Reframe how you think about evaluations. An evaluation is one person's perspective on a small sample of your teaching. It's feedback, and feedback can be useful, but it is not the final word on your competence. A less-than-perfect evaluation doesn't mean you're a bad teacher. It means there are areas where you can grow, which is true for every teacher at every stage of their career.

If you receive critical feedback, separate what is useful from what is not. Ask yourself:

- Is this feedback specific and actionable?
- Does it align with what I know about my students and my practice?
- Is this person seeing something I have missed, or are they applying a standard that doesn't fit my context?

Reflect on your growth regularly. At the end of each school year, take time to look back and notice how you've changed. What can you do now that you could not do a year ago? What feels easier? What are you less afraid of? Write it down. This reflection is not just a feel-good exercise. It's evidence of your competence, and you will need that evidence on the days when your confidence wavers.

Seek out feedback from people you trust. Not every piece of feedback is useful, but feedback from a mentor, a colleague you respect, or a coach who knows your work can help you see your strengths more clearly. Ask specific questions: What do you see me doing well? Where have you noticed me grow? What is one area where you think I could focus my development this year? Listen to the answers and let them shape your understanding of your own expertise.

Set small, achievable goals that build your confidence over time. Confidence grows when you set a goal, work toward it, and achieve it. The goal doesn't have to be big. It can be as simple as "I will try one new classroom management strategy this month" or "I will leave school by four o'clock three days this week." When you achieve the goal, you prove to yourself that you're capable of change and growth. That proof builds confidence for the next goal and the next.

You are building a career, not perfecting a performance. Every year you teach adds to your expertise, your confidence, and your capacity to make a difference. You do not have to have it all figured out today. You just have to keep showing up, keep learning, and keep trusting that you are exactly the teacher your students need.

You are not an imposter. You are a teacher who is still learning, still growing, and still making a difference every single day. The voice that tells you otherwise is not telling the truth. Silence it. Own what you know. Define success on your own terms. Build confidence that grows with every year you teach. You are enough, you are capable, and you are exactly where you are supposed to be.

Chapter 8. Building Your Sustainable Teaching Practice

Sustainability in teaching is about designing a practice that protects your energy, honors your boundaries, and allows you to show up fully present for your students without sacrificing yourself in the process.

You cannot pour from an empty cup, and teaching will drain every drop if you let it. The profession demands endless giving, but it rarely asks you to protect what you need to keep giving. That is why so many passionate teachers burn out before they ever reach their full potential. They give and give until there is nothing left.

But it doesn't have to be that way. You can create a teaching life that honors both your calling and your humanity.

Designing Daily and Weekly Routines That Protect Your Energy

The most sustainable teaching practices are built on routines that protect energy rather than deplete it. You can have all the time in the world and still feel exhausted if you're spending that time on tasks that drain you. The goal is to design daily and weekly routines that preserve your mental, emotional, and physical energy so you can show up for your students and for yourself.

Start by identifying your non-negotiables – the boundaries and routines that protect your wellbeing no matter what, and build your daily routine around these non-negotiables. These are not luxuries. They are necessities.

For some teachers, a non-negotiable is leaving school by 4:00 PM every day. For others, it's not checking email after 6:00 PM or taking one full day each weekend completely off from schoolwork. Your non-negotiables will be personal to you, but they must be clear and they must be protected.

If you know you need to leave by 4:00 PM, plan your day so that grading, planning, and administrative tasks happen during your planning period or before school rather than after. Use the AI tools you've learned to handle repetitive tasks like drafting emails, generating discussion questions, or creating exit tickets so you're not staying late to finish work that technology can do for you in minutes.

Create a weekly planning rhythm that reduces decision fatigue and protects your evenings. Dedicate one block of time each week – perhaps Sunday afternoon or Friday after school – to map out the week ahead. Review your curriculum map, confirm which lessons are coming up, and use AI to generate or refine any materials you need. When you walk into Monday morning with the entire week already planned, you eliminate the daily scramble that steals your energy and your peace of mind.

Protect your transition time. The moments between school and home are critical for your mental health. Whether it's a ten-minute drive, a walk around the block, or simply sitting in your car for five minutes before you go inside, give yourself a buffer between teacher mode and personal life. Use that time to decompress, to let go of the day, and to mentally shift into the next part of your life. Do not bring the weight of the classroom into your home every single night.

Design your week to include restorative activities that refill your energy rather than drain it. This might mean scheduling a workout class, a coffee date with a friend, or simply an evening with no plans at all.

You do not have to earn rest. You need rest to do the work well.

Pay attention to the tasks that drain you most and find ways to minimize or eliminate them.

- If grading essays exhausts you, use AI to provide initial feedback on grammar and structure so you can focus your energy on the meaningful content feedback only you can give.
- If parent communication feels overwhelming, create templates and use AI to draft responses so you're not starting from scratch every time.
- If lesson planning steals your weekends, batch your planning during the school week using your curriculum map and AI-generated resources.

When you design routines that honor your energy, you show up as a better teacher, a better colleague, and a better version of yourself.

Recognizing Early Warning Signs of Burnout Before It's Too Late

Burnout builds slowly, quietly, until one day you realize you have nothing left to give. The most important skill you can develop as a teacher is the ability to recognize the early warning signs of burnout before it becomes a crisis.

- **The first warning sign is physical exhaustion that doesn't improve with rest.** If you're sleeping enough but still waking up tired, if you're getting through the day on caffeine and willpower, if you feel physically drained even on weekends, your body is telling you something important. Listen to it. Physical exhaustion is not a badge of honor. It's a signal that something needs to change.

- **The second warning sign is emotional numbness or detachment.** If you find yourself going through the motions in the classroom without feeling the joy or connection that once fueled you, if you're irritable with students or colleagues over small things, if you feel cynical or resentful about teaching, you are experiencing emotional burnout. This is not a character flaw. It's a symptom of giving more than you have to give for too long.

- **The third warning sign is mental fog and decision fatigue.** If you're struggling to make even simple decisions, if you feel overwhelmed by tasks that used to feel manageable, if you cannot focus or remember things the way you used to, your mind is overloaded. Teaching requires thousands of decisions every single day, and when your mental energy is depleted, even the smallest choice feels impossible.

- **The fourth warning sign is withdrawal from relationships and activities you used to enjoy.** If you're canceling plans with friends, avoiding social events, or spending all your free time alone because you're too exhausted to engage, you are isolating yourself in a way that deepens burnout rather than relieves it. Connection is not optional. It's essential to your wellbeing.

- **The fifth warning sign is guilt that follows you everywhere.** If you feel guilty when you're working because you're not spending time with loved ones, and guilty when you're not working because you feel like you should be doing more for your students, you are trapped in a cycle that has no winning outcome. This kind of pervasive guilt is not motivating. It is paralyzing.

When you notice these warning signs, do not ignore them. Don't tell yourself you just need to push through until the next break. Burnout doesn't fix itself with a long weekend or a week off at Thanksgiving. It requires intentional intervention.

Start by naming what you are experiencing. Say it out loud to someone you trust. "I think I am burning out." Naming it removes some of its power and opens the door to getting support. Talk to a colleague, a mentor, a friend, or a therapist. You do not have to carry this alone.

Next, identify one thing you can change immediately. You do not have to overhaul your entire life, but you do need to take one concrete action that reduces your load.

- Maybe it's saying no to an extra committee.
- Maybe it's using AI to handle grading for one assignment.
- Maybe it's setting a firm boundary around your evenings.

Pick one thing and do it this week.

Finally, revisit your non-negotiables and recommit to them. Burnout often happens when boundaries erode slowly over time. You start staying a little later, checking email a little more often, saying yes to just one more thing. Before you know it, your non-negotiables are gone and you are running on empty. Protecting your boundaries is not selfish. It's the only way to sustain a long career in teaching.

Creating a Personalized Sustainability Plan That Evolves With You

Sustainability is not a one-size-fits-all formula. What works for a first-year teacher will not work for someone in year eight. What works during a calm semester will not work during a season of personal crisis. Your sustainability plan must be personalized to your life, your needs, and your season, and it must be flexible enough to evolve as you do.

Start by assessing where you are right now. Take an honest inventory of your current routines, boundaries, and energy levels.

- What is working?
- What is draining you?
- What do you need more of?
- What do you need less of?

Next, define what sustainability looks like for you personally. For some teachers, sustainability means leaving school by 4:00 PM every day and never working weekends. For others, it means having the flexibility to work Sunday afternoons but protecting Friday nights. For others, it means using AI to cut planning time in half so there is space for a hobby or a side project. There is no right answer. There is only your answer.

Build your sustainability plan around three core areas: time, energy, and boundaries.

- In the area of time, identify where you will use AI tools, curriculum mapping, and batching strategies to reclaim hours each week. Be specific. "I will use AI to generate discussion questions every Monday during my planning period." "I will batch-plan my lessons every Sunday from 2:00 to 4:00 PM using my curriculum map." Specificity turns intentions into actions.

- In the area of energy, identify what refills you and what drains you, and design your routines accordingly. If mornings are your high-energy time, protect them for your most important work. If you're drained by the end of the school day, do not schedule meetings or parent calls after school unless absolutely necessary. If grading depletes you, use AI to handle the repetitive parts so you can focus your energy on meaningful feedback.

- In the area of boundaries, define your non-negotiables and communicate them clearly. Boundaries only work if you honor them consistently and if the people around you understand them. If you do not work past 6:00 PM, turn off your email notifications and let colleagues know you will respond the next day. If you do not work Saturdays, protect that day fiercely and do not let guilt creep in.

Your sustainability plan should also include regular check-ins with yourself. Set a recurring calendar reminder once a month to assess how you are doing. Are your routines still working? Are your boundaries holding? Are you experiencing any early warning signs of burnout? If something is not working, adjust it. Sustainability is not about rigidity. It's about responsiveness.

Building a Teaching Practice That Lasts for Decades

The foundation of a decades-long teaching career is the belief that your wellbeing is not separate from your effectiveness as a teacher. You are not a better teacher when you sacrifice your health, your relationships, and your personal life. You are a better teacher when you're rested, supported, and whole. This is not a nice idea. It's a professional necessity.

Build your teaching practice around the tools and strategies that give you time and energy back. Use AI to handle the repetitive tasks that steal your evenings. Use curriculum mapping to eliminate daily decision fatigue and keep you on pace all year long. Use batching and templates to streamline your planning and communication. These are not shortcuts. They are the tools that make a long career possible.

Cultivate relationships with colleagues who support your sustainability rather than undermine it. Surround yourself with teachers who respect boundaries, who do not glorify overwork, and who remind you that leaving at a reasonable hour doesn't make you less dedicated. Distance yourself from the culture of martyrdom that says good teachers must suffer. That culture doesn't produce better teachers. It produces burnout and turnover.

Invest in your growth and development throughout your career. Attend workshops, read books, try new strategies, and stay curious. Teachers who continue learning and evolving are far less likely to burn out than those who feel stuck doing the same thing year after year. Growth doesn't have to mean more work. It can mean finding smarter, more efficient ways to do the work you're already doing.

Protect your summers and breaks as sacred time for rest and renewal. Do not spend your entire summer planning for the next school year. Do not spend your winter break catching up on grading. Use your curriculum map and AI tools to prepare in advance so your breaks can actually be breaks. You need time away from teaching to remember who you are outside of the classroom.

Revisit your why regularly. Why did you become a teacher? What do you love about this work? When you feel disconnected or discouraged, go back to that original calling. Spend time with students in ways that remind you why you chose this profession. Have a conversation that matters. Celebrate a breakthrough. Notice the small moments of connection that make teaching meaningful. Your why is the anchor that keeps you grounded when everything else feels chaotic.

Finally, give yourself permission to evolve as a teacher. You do not have to teach the same way in year fifteen that you taught in year one. You do not have to say yes to every opportunity or every request. You do not have to be everything to everyone. You can say no. You can set boundaries. You can change your mind. You can build a teaching practice that fits your life rather than forcing your life to fit your teaching practice.

A sustainable teaching career is not about perfection. It's about persistence. It's about showing up, doing your best, and knowing that your best will look different on different days. It's about building a practice that allows you to teach for decades without losing yourself in the process. It's about honoring both your calling and your humanity, and understanding that you cannot have one without the other.

Building a sustainable teaching practice is the most generous thing you can do – for your students, for your colleagues, for your loved ones, and for yourself. When you protect your energy, honor your boundaries, and design routines that support your wellbeing, you become the teacher you always wanted to be. Not because you're working harder, but because you're working smarter. Not because you're giving more, but because you're giving from a place of fullness rather than depletion.

Your teaching career can be long, fulfilling, and joyful. It can honor both your professional calling and your personal life. It can be sustainable. But only if you choose to make it so. The tools are in your hands. The plan is in place. Now it's time to build the teaching life you deserve.

Chapter 9. Thrive – Teaching as a Calling

You came into teaching to change lives, and somewhere along the way, you forgot that your life matters too. This final chapter is about reclaiming both – your impact on students and your right to a fulfilling life outside the classroom.

It's about understanding that thriving in teaching is not a destination you arrive at once and stay forever. It's a practice, a series of choices you make every single day to protect your energy, honor your calling, and remember that you matter just as much as the students you serve.

What a Thriving Teaching Career Actually Looks Like

A thriving teaching career doesn't mean every day is perfect. It doesn't mean you never feel tired, never have a difficult class, or never question a decision you made. Thriving doesn't mean the absence of challenge. It means having the tools, the mindset, and the support systems in place to meet those challenges without losing yourself in the process.

A thriving teacher leaves school most days at a reasonable hour. Not because she cares less about her students, but because she has learned to work smarter. She has systems in place that handle the repetitive tasks. She uses AI to draft lesson plans, generate assessments, and provide feedback so she can spend her energy on the human moments that matter most – the conversations with struggling students, the creative projects that light up her classroom, the connections that remind her why she became a teacher in the first place.

A thriving teacher has weekends that belong to her. She does not spend every Saturday grading papers or every Sunday planning the week ahead. She has built a curriculum map that guides her through the year so she is not reinventing the wheel every single week. She has a library of resources – many created with AI assistance – that she can pull from and adapt rather than starting from scratch. She has learned that rest is not a luxury. It's a requirement for doing this work well.

A thriving teacher sets boundaries without guilt. She doesn't answer parent emails at nine o'clock at night. She doesn't volunteer for every committee, chaperone every event, or say yes to every request that comes her way. She has learned that protecting her time and energy is not selfish – it's strategic. A teacher who is rested, balanced, and mentally healthy is far more effective than one who is running on fumes and resentment.

A thriving teacher measures success differently than she used to. She no longer defines her worth by test scores, administrator evaluations, or how many hours she works. She measures success by the quality of her relationships with students, by the moments of genuine learning and connection she witnesses, by her ability to show up fully present rather than completely depleted. She knows that the most important metric is whether she can sustain this work for the long haul without burning out.

A thriving teacher is not afraid of change. She doesn't panic when new initiatives are introduced or when technology evolves. She has learned to adapt, to experiment, and to use tools like AI to make transitions smoother rather than more stressful. She is confident in her ability to learn, to grow, and to navigate whatever comes next because she has done it before and she knows she can do it again.

A thriving teacher still loves teaching. Not every single day, but most days. She still feels the spark of purpose that brought her into this profession. She still believes she is making a difference. And most importantly, she believes she can keep doing this work for years to come without sacrificing her health, her relationships, or her sense of self.

Celebrating Your Transformation From Surviving to Thriving

Take a moment to acknowledge how far you've come. When you started this book, you may have been in survival mode – just trying to make it through each day, each week, each grading period. You may have been questioning whether you could continue teaching at all. You may have felt alone, under-equipped, and overwhelmed by a job that seemed designed to break you.

Now look at what you've built. You have a year-long curriculum map that gives you clarity and direction instead of constant decision fatigue. You know where you are going and how to get there. You are no longer scrambling week to week, wondering what to teach next or whether you are on pace. You have a roadmap, and that roadmap has given you something invaluable – peace of mind.

You've learned to use AI as your teaching assistant. What once felt intimidating or even threatening now feels like a lifeline. You have used AI to generate lesson plans, create assessments, draft parent communications, and provide student feedback. You have saved hours every single week – hours you've given back to yourself. Hours you've spent with your family, pursuing hobbies, resting, or simply doing nothing at all. You have proven to yourself that you do not have to choose between being a great teacher and having a personal life.

You've set boundaries that protect your well-being. You've learned to say no. You've learned to leave work at work most days. You've learned that guilt is not a useful emotion when it comes to self-care. You've given yourself permission to rest, to recharge, and to show up as a whole person rather than an exhausted shell of who you used to be.

You've reconnected with your purpose. Somewhere in the process of learning new tools and building new systems, you remembered why you became a teacher. You remembered the students. You remembered the moments that matter. You remembered that teaching is not about perfection – it's about connection, growth, and showing up day after day with intention and care.

This transformation did not happen because you worked harder. It happened because you worked smarter. It happened because you were willing to try something new, to learn tools that felt unfamiliar, and to challenge the belief that suffering is a requirement for being a good teacher. You have proven that there is another way. A better way. A sustainable way.

You are not the same teacher you were when you started this journey. You are stronger, more resourceful, and more confident. You are equipped. And that changes everything.

Weathering Future Challenges With Your New Tools and Mindset

Teaching will always come with challenges. That is the nature of the work. There will be difficult students, demanding parents, shifting policies, new initiatives, budget cuts, and moments when you question whether anything you're doing is making a difference. Those challenges have not disappeared just because you have new tools and systems in place.

But you now have the capacity to weather those challenges without breaking. You've built a foundation that can absorb the shocks and stresses of teaching without collapsing. You have systems that keep you organized even when everything else feels chaotic. You have tools that save you time even when new demands are added to your plate. You have boundaries that protect your well-being even when the pressure intensifies.

When a new curriculum is introduced mid-year, you will not panic. You will open your curriculum map, adjust your pacing, and use AI to help you adapt your lesson plans quickly. What used to feel like starting over from scratch will now feel like a manageable adjustment. You have the tools to pivot without losing your footing.

When a particularly challenging class tests your patience and your sanity, you will not spiral into self-doubt. You will remember that difficult classes are part of teaching, not evidence that you're failing. You will use the strategies you've learned to manage behavior, engage reluctant learners, and protect your energy. You will reach out for support when you need it instead of suffering in silence. You will remind yourself that one hard class doesn't define your entire career.

When the workload feels overwhelming again – and it will, because teaching is cyclical and some seasons are harder than others – you will not revert to bringing work home every night. You will look at your systems, identify what is taking up the most time, and use AI to streamline those tasks. You will prioritize what actually matters and let go of what does not. You will protect your evenings and weekends because you've learned that rest is not optional.

When burnout starts creeping back in – and you will recognize the signs now because you know what to look for – you will not push through until you break. You will pause, reassess, and make adjustments. You will revisit the boundaries you've set and strengthen them if needed. You will remind yourself that taking care of yourself is not selfish – it's the only way to sustain this work.

When new technology emerges or when AI evolves in ways you did not expect, you will not be intimidated. You've already proven to yourself that you can learn new tools and adapt to change. You will approach new technology with curiosity rather than fear. You will experiment, ask questions, and figure out how to make it work for you rather than against you.

The difference between surviving and thriving is not that thriving teachers never face challenges. It's that they have the tools, the mindset, and the support systems to face those challenges without losing themselves. You've built that foundation. You've equipped yourself. And that means you're ready for whatever comes next.

Conclusion

The teacher who picked up this book at the beginning was likely exhausted, overwhelmed, and quietly wondering if teaching could ever feel sustainable. That teacher was carrying too much – not because of a lack of dedication, but because of a lack of tools. The weight of lesson planning, grading, parent communication, and administrative tasks had become so heavy that the joy of teaching was buried underneath it all.

If that was you, something has shifted by now. Not because the demands of teaching have magically disappeared, but because you now have something you did not have before: a clear roadmap for reclaiming your time, your energy, and your life outside the classroom.

The question that brought you here was simple and urgent: How do I stop bringing work home every night? The answer, as you have discovered, is not about working harder or becoming more efficient through sheer willpower. The answer is about being equipped. It's about using the right tools – specifically AI – to handle the repetitive, time-consuming tasks that drain you, so you can focus your human energy on the moments that actually matter. The moments when a student finally understands a difficult concept. The moments when you notice a quiet kid starting to open up. The moments when your classroom feels less like a checklist and more like a community.

AI is not a replacement for you. It never will be. But it's the assistant you have always needed and never had. It can draft your lesson plans, generate your assessments, write your parent emails, and provide personalized feedback to students – all in a fraction of the time it would take you to do it manually. And when you use it responsibly and ethically, it doesn't compromise your integrity as an educator. It amplifies your impact.

You also arrived with a fear that needed to be addressed before you could move forward: Is AI safe and ethical to use in my classroom? That fear was valid. Any tool this powerful deserves careful consideration, especially in education where trust, privacy, and student wellbeing are paramount. But as you've learned, AI is not inherently dangerous. It is a tool, and like any tool, it can be used responsibly or recklessly. The difference lies in how you use it.

When you use AI to save time on administrative tasks, you're not cutting corners – you're being strategic. When you use it to generate ideas and then personalize them for your students, you're not being lazy – you're being resourceful. When you set boundaries around student data, review everything AI produces, and maintain your role as the decision-maker in your classroom, you are using AI exactly the way it was meant to be used: as a support system, not a substitute.

The educators who thrive in the years ahead will not be the ones who resist change or cling to outdated methods out of fear. They will be the ones who adapt, who learn, and who use every available resource to protect their energy and sustain their passion. You are now one of those educators.

But perhaps the most important question this book has addressed is the one you were afraid to say out loud: How do I set boundaries without feeling guilty? This question cuts deeper than time management or technology. It strikes at the heart of what so many teachers believe about themselves – that being a good teacher means giving everything, sacrificing everything, and never saying no.

That belief is a lie. And it is a dangerous one.

You cannot pour from an empty cup. You cannot show up fully for your students if you're running on fumes. You cannot sustain a 20-year career if you burn out in year five. And you cannot be the educator your students need if you've lost yourself in the process.

Setting boundaries is not selfish. It's not a sign of weakness or a lack of commitment. It's a professional necessity. When you protect your evenings, your weekends, and your personal life, you're not abandoning your students – you're ensuring that you will still be there for them tomorrow, next month, and next year. You are modeling for them what it looks like to live a balanced, healthy, sustainable life. And that lesson is just as important as anything you will ever teach them from a textbook.

The guilt you've been carrying doesn't serve you or your students. It's time to let it go.

This book has given you three things that will change the trajectory of your teaching career if you use them.

First, you now have a year-long curriculum mapping system that removes the daily decision fatigue and keeps you on pace without the constant panic of falling behind. You know how to see the big picture, build in flexibility for the unexpected, and prioritize what actually matters. You are no longer planning week to week, scrambling to stay one day ahead of your students. You have a roadmap, and that roadmap gives you clarity, confidence, and control.

Second, you now have a practical understanding of AI and exactly how to use it to save hours every single week. You know which tools to use, how to use them step by step, and how to integrate them into your workflow without feeling overwhelmed. You know how to write better lesson plans faster, generate assessments that actually measure understanding, communicate with parents without spending your evenings drafting emails, and provide meaningful feedback to students without drowning in grading. You are no longer intimidated by technology. You are empowered by it.

Third, and most importantly, you now have permission to protect your personal life and the strategies to actually do it. You know how to recognize the early warning signs of burnout before it becomes a crisis. You know how to set boundaries that honor both your students and yourself. You know how to measure your success in ways that matter beyond test scores and administrative metrics. You know that your worth as a teacher is not determined by how many hours you work or how much you sacrifice. Your worth is determined by the relationships you build, the growth you inspire, and the sustainability you create.

These three pillars – planning, technology, and boundaries – are not separate strategies. They work together. When you plan well, you reduce stress. When you use AI effectively, you reclaim time. When you set boundaries, you protect your energy. And when you protect your energy, you show up as the teacher you always wanted to be.

The teacher who finishes this book is not the same teacher who started it. That teacher was surviving. You are now equipped to thrive.

But being equipped is not a one-time event. It is an ongoing practice. The tools in this book will only transform your career if you actually use them. So start small. Pick one AI tool and use it this week. Block out one evening where you do not bring work home. Build one unit of your curriculum map. Take one step, and then another, and then another. Transformation does not happen overnight, but it does happen – one intentional choice at a time.

You will have hard days. There will be weeks when the lesson doesn't go as planned, when the technology doesn't cooperate, when a parent sends a frustrating email, or when you question whether any of this is making a difference. In those moments, come back to this: You are not failing. You are human. And being human in a profession that demands so much is not a weakness – it is a testament to your strength.

You chose teaching because you believed you could make a difference. You still can. But you cannot make that difference if you disappear in the process. The students who need you most need you to stay – not just this year, but for the long haul. They need you healthy, rested, passionate, and present. They need the version of you that has a life outside of school, hobbies that bring you joy, relationships that fill you up, and boundaries that protect your wellbeing.

That version of you is not a luxury. It is the goal.

This book has handed you the tools to build a teaching career that doesn't require you to sacrifice your life. A career where you leave school at a reasonable hour, enjoy your weekends, and wake up on Monday morning without dread. A career where you use technology to work smarter, not harder. A career where you feel confident, capable, and in control. A career that lasts not because you're surviving, but because you are thriving.

You did not have to choose between being a great teacher and having a great life. You just did not have the right tools yet. Now you do.

So go build the career you deserve. The one where you make a difference in the lives of your students without losing yourself. The one where you use every resource available to protect your time and energy. The one where you set boundaries without guilt and show up fully without burning out.

Your students need you. But you need you too. And now, finally, you have what it takes to honor both.

The teaching profession needs educators like you – passionate, dedicated, and willing to adapt. But it needs you whole, not broken. It needs you equipped, not just inspired. It needs you for the long haul.

Welcome to the rest of your teaching career. It starts now!

Thank You for Reading!

I hope you found **The AI-Equipped Teacher** helpful and enjoyable!

Your feedback is invaluable to me and helps others discover this book.

If you could take a moment to leave a review, I'd greatly appreciate it. Scan the QR code below to leave your review:

Thank you!

Patty

Visit the Cantelune Press website for more compassionate books that meet you where you are! https://cantelunepress.com/

Bibliography

References

Chambers, C. (2025, July 24). *What a New Survey Says About Teachers' Plans to Leave Their Jobs*. NEA Today.

EduStaff. (2026, February 3). *Teacher Shortages in 2025: What the Data Revealed and What 2026 Will Demand*. EduStaff.

Aston Education. (n.d.). *Teacher burnout in 2026: what's improved and what hasn't*. Aston Education.

Tan, T. S., Wei, W., Carver-Thomas, D., & García, E. (2026, March 17). *Teacher Turnover in the United States: Who Moves, Who Leaves, and Why*. Learning Policy Institute.

The Hartford Staff. (2026, January 02). *Teacher Burnout: Supporting and Retaining Employees in the Education Sector*. The Hartford.

The ATLIS. (n.d.). *Harnessing AI to Prevent Teacher Burnout*. The ATLIS Resources.

Nittle, N. (August 13, 2025). *Could AI prevent teacher burnout?*. The 19th.

Grade with AI. (n.d.). *Page not found*. Grade with AI.

Grimes, J. (2026, February 10). *How district leaders can address teacher burnout before it impacts student outcomes*. SchoolAI.

Colleague.ai. (2024, September 22). *The Burning Issue: Understanding Teacher Burnout and How Colleague AI Can Help*. Colleague.ai.

Miller, M. (n.d.). *Discover AI for Educators*. Ditch That Textbook.

Bowen, J. A., & Watson, C. E. (2024, April 30). *Teaching with AI: A Practical Guide to a New Era of Human Learning*. Goodreads.

Sturgill, A. (2024, September 19). *Book Review: Teaching with AI*. Center for Engaged Learning.

Buyserie, B., & Thurston, T. N. (2024). *Teaching and Generative AI: Pedagogical Possibilities and Productive Tensions*. Utah State University.

Bowen, J. A., & Watson, C. E. (2024, April 30). *Teaching with AI: A Practical Guide to a New Era of Human Learning*. Goodreads.

Bowen, J. A., & Watson, C. E. (n.d.). *Teaching with AI*. Winkist.

The AI Educator. (n.d.). *The AI Classroom*. The AI Educator.

Hewett, V. (n.d.). *Teacher burnout and how to avoid it*. Education Support.

AASPA. (2025, March 5). *How to Avoid Teacher Burnout and Increase Teacher Retention (2025)*. American Association of School Personnel Administrators.

Lighston, H. J. (2021, November). *Preventing and addressing teacher burnout: Why resilience and growth mindset matter for educators*. Leadership Magazine.

PowerSchool. (n.d.). *Teacher Burnout Prevention Strategies*. PowerSchool.

Provenzano, N. (n.d.). *Roll With It: Burnout Prevention*. Edutopia.

Walker, T. (2021, November 12). *Getting Serious About Teacher Burnout*. NEA Today.

Nuzum, S. (2025, April 30). *Teacher Exhaustion and Burnout*. The South Carolina Education Association.

Ithaca College. (n.d.). *Burnout and Other Emotional Exhaustions for Teachers*. Ithaca College.

Stevens, G. (2023, November 22). *The Science Behind Teacher Burnout versus Compassion Fatigue for Teachers*. Grace Stevens.

Cox, J. (2025, February 27). *Beyond Tired: Recognizing Teacher Burnout Symptoms*. TeachHub.

Jones, A. (2025, February 4). *From Burnout to Balance: Understanding and Preventing Teacher Burnout*. Kappa Delta Pi.

EduStaff. (2025, October 22). *Teacher Burnout: How to Recognize It and Rekindle the Spark*. EduStaff.

Cahill, B. (December 23, 2025). *Teacher Burnout: What It Is, Key Statistics, Symptoms, and Prevention Strategies*. Discovery Education.

Faria, S. (2022, June 4). *Back from Burnout: 4 Tips for Renewing Your Passion*. Teaching Strategies.

Inventors & Makers. (n.d.). *Teacher Burnout Recovery*. Inventors & Makers.

Blackwell, B. (2024, February 6). 92. *How to Hack Your Teacher Brain to Beat Burnout: Neuroscience Strategies to Reignite Your Passion*. Teaching Mind Body and Soul.

University of San Diego Professional & Continuing Education. (n.d.). *15 Ways to Prevent Teacher Burnout [+ FAQs]*. University of San Diego Professional & Continuing Education.

The Muse. (2024, December 10). *Teacher Burnout: How to Recognize, Prevent, and Overcome It*. Pittsburg State University Career Development.

Gaughan, A. (2025, May 13). *What to Do If You're Experiencing Teacher Burnout*. Moreland University.

PowerSchool. (n.d.). *The Benefits of Curriculum Mapping*. PowerSchool.

RIS Center. (n.d.). *Page 13: Year-long Planning*. IRIS Center.

DeFlitch, S. (n.d.). *How Curriculum Mapping and Lesson Planning Save Time*. Panorama Education.

Crocco, L. (n.d.). *Benefits of curriculum mapping for teaching efficiency and program management*. Teaching@Sydney.

Edusfere. (2025, May 3). *How are Teachers using Curriculum Mapping to Design More Effective Lessons?*. Edusfere.

Rodgers, A. (n.d.). *Curriculum Map Template Key Benefits of Effective Curriculum Mapping*. Education Advanced.

Kallick, K. T. (2006, December 7). *Curriculum Mapping A Step-by-Step Guide for Creating Curriculum Year Overviews*. ERIC.

Tunnell, K. (n.d.). *Curriculum Mapping: 4 Steps to Implement*. Education Advanced.

Mezni, A. (2024, September 8). *How to Make a Curriculum Map: Step by Step Guide for Teachers*. Teaching Ideas 4U.

Sing to Kids. (2023, July 29). *Curriculum Mapping Made Easy*. Sing to Kids.

Treehouse Schoolhouse. (2025, May 29). *Our Homeschool Daily Rhythms Over the Years*. Treehouse Schoolhouse.

Teachers Pay Teachers. (n.d.). *Curriculum Maps*. Teachers Pay Teachers.

Sackstein, S. (2018, July 24). *Writing a Flexible Curricular Map to Ensure Student Voice is Heard*. Education Week.

Main, P. (2024, February 1). *Curriculum Mapping: A Teacher's Guide*. Structural Learning.

Atlas. (2022, July 31). *Supporting New Teachers: Building a Purpose for Curriculum Mapping*. Atlas.

Center for Excellence in Teaching, Learning and Innovation. (2022, February 22). *Combining Structure and Flexibility in Your Courses*. Center for Excellence in Teaching, Learning and Innovation.

EI. (2025, September 24). *A Guide to Curriculum Mapping for L&D Leaders*. EI Design.

Nicola K. (2023, July 17). *Curriculum Mapping: A Comprehensive Guide for Teachers*. Teach Simple.

Okojie, M. U., Bastas, M., & Miralay, F. (2022, August 18). *Using Curriculum Mapping as a Tool to Match Student Learning Outcomes and Social Studies Curricula*. Frontiers in Psychology.

Magnet ABA. (n.d.). *Setting the Stage for Success in Education Through Organized Calendars and Time Management*. Magnet ABA.

Bradbury, J. D. (n.d.). *Calendar Management Strategies for Instructional Coaches*. TeacherCast.

Curriculum Associates. (n.d.). *Strategies for Time Management for Teachers*. Curriculum Associates.

Ellis, M. (n.d.). *Time-blocking for teachers and trainers: manage your time to improve your wellbeing*. SET.

GraduateProgram.org. (n.d.). *Time Management Tips for Busy Teachers*. GraduateProgram.org.

EAB. (March 5, 2021). *How to catch students up in less time: 6 strategies to expedite learning recovery*. EAB.

Butler, B. (2022, November 11). *A Strategy for Learning Recovery*. Teaching Channel.

Diaz, A. (n.d.). *3 Strategic Actions to Learning Recovery*. Amira Learning.

Gillyard, A. (n.d.). *3 Ways Lesson Plans Flop – and How to Recover*. Edutopia.

Education Resource Strategies. (n.d.). *Tending Gardens & Putting Out Fires*. Education Resource Strategies.

Minkel, J. (2017, March 07). *A Teacher's Pursuit of Imperfection*. Education Week.

Edutopia. (n.d.). *Small but Impactful Classroom Management Shifts*. Edutopia.

Warner Pacific University. (2025, September 17). *7 Classroom Management Strategies for Teachers*. Warner Pacific University.

Zeldin, I. (2025, February 11). *How to Make Imperfect Decisions*. 2gnoMe.

Edutopia. (n.d.). *The Trouble With Perfectionism in Teaching*. Edutopia.

Teach Starter. (n.d.). *11 Easy Ways to Help Students Manage Perfectionism*. Teach Starter.

Point Loma Nazarene University. (n.d.). *5 Ways to Prevent Burnout as a Teacher*. Point Loma Nazarene University.

Edutopia. (n.d.). *How New Teachers Can Avoid Burnout*. Edutopia.

Chroma Early Learning Academy. (2025, December 26). *Effective Strategies for Preventing Teacher Burnout: Ensuring Early Childhood Educator Well-Being and Retention*. Chroma Early Learning Academy.

NASA. (n.d.). *What is Artificial Intelligence?*. NASA.

Coursera Staff. (2026, March 13). *What Is Artificial Intelligence? Definition, Uses, and Types*. Coursera.

Google Cloud. (n.d.). *Artificial intelligence (AI): a simple-to-understand guide*. Google Cloud.

University of Notre Dame. (n.d.). *AI Overview and Definitions*. AI for Teaching and Learning.

Monahan, J. (2023, July). *Artificial Intelligence, Explained*. CMU Heinz College.

Wikipedia. (n.d.). *Artificial intelligence*. Wikipedia.

Pattam, A. (2021, September 16). *Artificial Intelligence, defined in simple terms*. HCLTech.

DeFlitch, S. (n.d.). *Misconceptions About AI in Education*. Panorama Education.

Walden University. (n.d.). *Access Denied - WAF Rule Reached*. ScholarWorks.

Harwick, R. (2025, October 8). *Debunking the Biggest Myths About Using AI in Education: A Teacher's Perspective*. Moreland University.

Digital Learning Institute. (n.d.). *6 Myths about AI in Learning*. Digital Learning Institute.

Blocksi. (n.d.). *5 Common Misconceptions on AI in Education: Have You Heard of H-AI-H?*. Blocksi.

TeachBetter.ai. (2025, February 2). *AI in Education: Busting Common Myths*. The Knowledge Hub.

EdTech Magazine. (2025, March). *AI-Powered Teaching Assistants*. EdTech Magazine.

Healey, M. (2025, December 9). *The Pros and Cons of AI in Education: Benefits, Risks, and Real Examples*. Discovery Education.

Cancellieri, P. (January 31, 2024). *Perspective | Artificial intelligence as a promising teacher assistant*. EdNC.

Klein, E. (2025, June 20). *Revolutionize Your Classroom: The Ultimate Guide to AI Tools for Teachers*. American College of Education.

Li Haoyang, D., & Towne, J. (2025, January). *How AI and human teachers can collaborate to transform education*. World Economic Forum.

Prothero, A. (August 20, 2025). *Are AI Teacher Assistants Reliable? What to Know*. Education Week.

Burns, M., & Winthrop, R. (2026, January 14). *AI's future for students is in our hands*. Brookings Institution.

Vilcarino, J. (2026, January 30). *The Risks and Rewards of AI in School: What to Know*. Education Week.

Freitag, E. (2025, December 18). *Some predictions about AI in education in 2026*. Thomas B. Fordham Institute.

Seril, L. (2026, March 3). *25 AI in Education Statistics to Guide Your Learning Strategy in 2026*. Engageli Blog.

United States Artificial Intelligence Institute. (2025, October 06). *Part 1: AI in Education, Classroom Integration, and Impact in 2026*. United States Artificial Intelligence Institute.

Office of Communications, College of Education. (2024, October 24). *AI in Schools: Pros and Cons*. College of Education.

Pawar, D. (2026, January 14). *AI in Education: Real Use Cases, Benefits, Limits, and What It Means in Practice*. Mitr Media.

U.S. Department of Education. (n.d.). *34 CFR Part 99 – Family Educational Rights and Privacy*. Student Privacy Policy Office.

California Department of Education. (2025, April 22). *FERPA Summary Page*. California Department of Education.

U.S. Department of Education. (n.d.). *What is FERPA*. Student Privacy.

California Health Sciences University. (n.d.). *Family Educational Right and Privacy Act (FERPA)*. California Health Sciences University.

U.S. Department of Education. (n.d.). *What must consent to disclose education records contain*. Student Privacy Policy Office.

EPIC. (n.d.). *Family Educational Rights and Privacy Act (FERPA)*. EPIC.

Nason, A. (2024, March 05). *Guide to FERPA Compliance for Schools*. Coro.

Ross, L. (n.d.). *Family Educational Rights and Privacy Act (FERPA) Compliance: A Complete Guide*. BigID.

Montclair State University. (2026, February 13). *AI Tools and Data Privacy*. Phish Files.

National Education Association. (June 20, 2025). *Student and Educator Data Privacy*. National Education Association.

MIT Sloan Teaching & Learning Technologies. (n.d.). *Navigating Data Privacy*. MIT Sloan Educational Technology.

UCO IT. (2024, October 20). *Protecting Your Data When Using AI Tools*. UCO IT Blog.

Security Journey. (December 19, 2024). *5 Types of Data You Should NEVER Share with AI*. Security Journey.

Soares, W. (December 13, 2024). *AI tools and student data: Teachers can endanger kids' privacy without robust training*. Chalkbeat.

Graf, J. (n.d.). *How to Protect Student Data from Hidden AI Risks*. CESA 6.

Mueller-Harder, T. (2023, August 25). *Protecting Information When Using AI Tools*. Brown University OIT Service Center.

Werra, E. (2026, March 01). *School Districts Are Writing Thoughtful AI Policies. What Does that Look Like?*. Skyward.

Hao, W. (2026, February). *States Take Next Steps on Governing AI Use in Schools*. NASBE.

Kosta, D. (2025, January 21). *State AI Guidance for K12 Schools*. AI for Education.

News Staff. (2026, January 08). *Ohio Unveils Model AI Policy for Use by K-12 Schools*. GovTech.

Newcomb, A. (2025, August 26). *From Suggestion to Requirement: K-12 School District AI Policy in 2025*. Agile Education Marketing.

Boxlight. (n.d.). *2026 Strategic Planning Guide*. Boxlight.

Bok Center for Teaching and Learning. (n.d.). *Examples & Ideas for Using AI for Your Teaching*. Bok Center for Teaching and Learning.

University of North Carolina at Charlotte. (n.d.). *Classroom Strategies to Promote Responsible Use of A.I.* UNC Charlotte Teaching.

Edutopia. (n.d.). *Teaching Students to Use AI Responsibly*. Edutopia.

Inspiring Teachers. (2025, August 12). *Modeling Responsible Artificial Intelligence (AI) in the Classroom*. Rutgers Alternate Route.

University of San Diego. (n.d.). *39 Examples of Artificial Intelligence in Education*. USD Online Degrees.

Lcom Team. (2025, August 31). *Creative & Responsible AI Classroom Activities for K–12*. Learning.com.

Muncey, N. (2025, June 24). *What responsible AI in education looks like and how to implement it*. SchoolAI.

Watson, A. (2024, September 22). *Teach students how to use artificial intelligence responsibly*. Truth for Teachers.

Leung, A. (2017, September 18). *Why do teachers feel guilty when they look after themselves?*. Alice Leung.

Álvarez, B. (November 15, 2024). *Say Goodbye to Teacher Guilt*. NEA Today.

How, L. (n.d.). *How often do you feel guilty?*. Education Support.

Teacher Transition. (2024, September 21). *Why Good Teachers Quit & Why They Shouldn't Feel Guilty*. Teacher Transition.

Dreaming Teachers. (2020, January 22). *Teacher Guilt*. Dreaming Teachers.

TeacherCareerCoach. (n.d.). *Battling Teacher Guilt About Leaving the Classroom*. Teacher Career Coach.

Elia, S. (2024, March 06). *'I Was Determined to Make a Change': A Teacher's Checklist for Work-Life Balance*. Education Week.

Edutopia. (n.d.). *Work-Life Balance for Teachers*. Edutopia.

Education Support. (n.d.). *Getting the right work-life balance*. Education Support.

NEA Member Benefits. (n.d.). *6 Ways to Create Work-Life Balance*. NEA Member Benefits.

Ferguson, M. (n.d.). *10 Habits of Teachers Who Nail Work-Life Balance*. Bored Teachers.

Markowitz, S. (n.d.). *Teacher Work Life Balance*. Progress Learning.

Caceres, C. (2025, March 18). *How to prioritise work-life balance in a demanding school environment*. T4 Education.

Watson, A. (2019, November 17). *How one teacher set boundaries and stopped bringing work home*. Truth for Teachers.

Edutopia. (n.d.). *Setting Healthy Emotional Boundaries for New Teachers*. Edutopia.

Sponaugle, E. (n.d.). *5 Ways Teachers Can Set Boundaries*. Erin Sponaugle.

Baylis, L. (n.d.). *How to Set Boundaries as an Overworked Educator*. Greater Good Magazine.

Wyrick, A. (2022, August 29). *How to Define Boundaries with Your Students – and Stick to Them*. Harvard Business Impact Education.

Smith, K. (2022, August 25). *How do I set boundaries for student-teacher interaction after school?*. Chalkbeat.

The Present Teacher. (2026, February 19). *Why You're Being Judged for Setting Boundaries as a Teacher*. The Present Teacher Blog.

www.ingramcontent.com/pod-product-compliance
Lightning Source LLC
Chambersburg PA
CBHW051809050726
47598CB00006B/2485

You became a teacher to change lives. Not to lose yours.

You're grading papers at midnight. You're planning lessons on Sunday mornings. You're exhausted before the week even begins – and somewhere beneath the pile of parent emails and data entry, the passionate teacher you once were is barely breathing.

You are not failing. You are under-equipped.

The AI-Equipped Teacher is the book the education system never gave you – a practical, compassionate roadmap for reclaiming your time, rebuilding your energy, and finally building the sustainable teaching career you deserve.

Inside, you'll discover:

- How to use AI tools to save 5–8 hours every single week – without compromising your integrity or your students

- Which AI platforms are actually worth your time (and exactly how to use them – zero tech experience required)

- How to build a year-long curriculum map that eliminates Sunday night panic for good

- The real difference between exhaustion and burnout – and what to do when rest stops working

- How to protect your personal life and become the teacher your students need

This isn't about working harder. It's about working equipped.

Whether you're three years in and already questioning your choice, or fifteen years in and running on fumes, this book will hand you the tools to stop surviving your career – and start loving it again.

Your evenings belong to you. Let's get them back!